THE OPEN BRAND

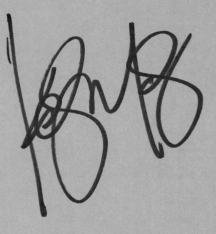

THE OPEN BRAND

WHEN PUSH COMES TO PULL IN
A WEB-MADE WORLD

Kelly Mooney and Dr. Nita Rollins

New Riders
1249 Eighth Street
Berkeley, CA 94710
510/524-2178
800/283-9444
510/524-2221 (fax)

Published in association with AIGA Design Press.

Find us on the Web at: www.newriders.com
To report errors, please send a note to
errata@peachpit.com

New Riders is an imprint of Peachpit,
a division of Pearson Education

Project Editor: Michael J. Nolan
Indexer: Julie Bess
Cover design: Base Art Co.
Interior design: Base Art Co.

ISBN 13: 978-0-321-54423-0
ISBN 10: 0-321-54423-4

9 8 7 6 5 4 3 2 1

Printed and bound in the United States of America

When Push Comes to Pull in a Web-Made World

Contents

Foreword

The early years in life, and in the life of a company, are the most formative. Our company, Resource Interactive, is no exception. Our beginnings trace back to 1981, when I took my first trip to Silicon Valley to visit our first client, a startup company by the name of Apple Computer. This first meeting, at their request, was to discuss whether we wanted to work with Apple to promote a new piece of consumer technology—the personal computer—which was being launched into retail computer stores around the country.

I left Apple's office that day, having found our first national client, and drove to Half Moon Bay on Highway 1, where I would spend the rest of the afternoon staring out at the Pacific Ocean daydreaming about how the company and technology I had just seen would change the world. Since that day, over 25 years ago, our associates have traveled to and worked in Silicon Valley—and all over the country—for Apple and other technology giants, and, increasingly, for some of the world's leading consumer brands. Along the way we have had a small hand in positioning or promoting everything from the first desktop publishing solution to the first flat rate pricing-based internet service, from the first lingerie fashion web cast to the first online community for snowboarders.

Throughout this entire professional journey, as a company and as individuals, we've always believed in the transformative power of Apple's earliest start-up mantra—"one person, one computer." Looking back, it's hard to dispute the fact that technology has become the great equalizer, propelling us into an age of connectivity and access that is unprecedented in human history.

Today, the single most powerful technology is a mashup of the World Wide Web and the open source movement. This power couple's ability to literally open up the world to us (think Google), while also allowing us to open up ourselves to the world (think

Facebook) dramatically impacts every business, every brand, and everyone. And it is because of the significance of the web as a democratizing change agent that we devoted our company's energies to crafting *The Open Brand*. My incredibly talented business partner, Kelly Mooney, along with the scholarly mind of our own Dr. Nita Rollins, were at the project's helm, while dozens of other Resource associates and friends helped research and develop the compelling content of the following pages. Our deep digital expertise, developed over a quarter of a century and influenced greatly by our early years in the business, will provide CEOs, Chief Marketing Officers, and hopefully, Chief Opening Officers (!) with a unique perspective that is both provocative and highly valuable.

I am proud to announce that Resource Interactive will donate all proceeds from book sales to the non-profit organization One Laptop Per Child (OLPC), so that one day all children can participate in and learn from the open global community online and, ultimately, import its opportunities and advantages to their own developing countries.

Nancy Kramer
Founder and CEO, Resource Interactive

Introduction

Five years ago, my first book, *The Ten Demandments: Rules to Live by in the Age of the Demanding Consumer*, was published. Resource Interactive, the interactive marketing firm where I am President, was an early advocate of consumer-centric, multichannel marketing, and *The Ten Demandments* highlighted what we perceived to be consumers' growing expectations—due to their internet empowerment—to dictate marketplace dynamics.

The Open Brand: When Push Comes to Pull in a Web-Made World continues charting the same trajectory of consumer empowerment. It examines what few could have predicted: the extent of consumers' overwhelming motivation for and adeptness at being heard, making a mark, controlling their experiences, shaping products, and sharing opinions. As the millennium turned, and marketers were recoiling and recovering from the dot.com bust, consumers remained unfazed—they were too busy experimenting with and embracing the internet. They adopted and customized new online tools and transformed the digital space into a profoundly social ecosystem they could create, control and own.

The media took note of this new breed of creative consumer—these "icitizens," as we've dubbed them. *TIME Magazine* crowned "You," the online consumer, its 2006 "Person of the Year." *Ad Age* chose the consumer as the "Agency of the Year." Marketers have to rethink their approach in the face of the mounting power and reach of consumers—both as individuals and communities. They must study the playbooks of icitizens who are using the internet and wireless devices to interact with and influence a vast social mesh of consumers. They must learn a new kind of brand management—of controls, not control—that inspires collaboration with and among consumers while still preserving the brand's essence.

Brands are already shifting away from reliance upon the 30-second spot that pushes predetermined messages to the consumer. The next step is to stage and support experiences that pull consumers into brand participation in a way that's relevant to their lives. Brands need to be open to forming multidimensional relationships with their consumers by accommodating all the ways they're using DIY tools on the web and wireless devices to create, share and influence brands—and each other. Brands, perhaps most importantly, need to tap consumers to co-create their future.

To relate to this authoritative new consumer who creates, shares and influences via the social web, a brand must be O.P.E.N.— on-demand, personal, engaging and networked. Open branding requires a cultural shift within every company to clearly understand and embrace this new reality. Openness needs new talent, new thinking, new models, new risks—and new interpretations of ROI.

Written with my colleague, Dr. Nita Rollins, as well as over forty Resource Interactive (RI) associates, *The Open Brand: When Push Comes to Pull in a Web-Made World* is the new strategic imperative for marketers and business executives. It frames an overarching trend and provides a shared language for cross-functional teams to engage in an immediate, tactical, open discussion about the future of your brand.

It is my hope that *The Open Brand* will make social web-empowered consumers and their web-made world an open book—comprehensible and compelling as the future of marketing. In keeping with the web's participatory ethos, I also sincerely hope you will share your open branding stories with RI and other marketers and brand enthusiasts at www.theopenbrand.com or theopenbrand@resource.com.

Kelly Mooney
President, Resource Interactive

Are you danger

ously CLOSED?

Do You Believe...?

Companies use marketing to control their message.

Brand managers own and orchestrate the brand.

Merchants dictate the product or service assortment.

Consumers buy what marketers promote.

Feedback only happens when brands invite it.

Ideas that matter come from the brand.

TV is where all marketing begins.

The web is for extending campaigns
(if there's leftover budget).

YouTube is a fad.

Online chatter is white noise.

Mobile phones are for making phone calls.

Bloggers are amateurs who should stick to their day jobs.

OR Do You Believe...?

- Consumers influence the messages marketers send.

- Consumers co-create brands.

- Consumers' opinions dictate the assortment.

- Consumers buy what their friends endorse.

- Consumers give feedback, expect to be heard and make noise if they're not.

- Consumers have ideas that matter to other consumers.

- Consumers view TV commercials as TiVo fodder.

- Consumers start with the web or end with the web—and increasingly do both.

- Consumers love YouTube because they think their content is better than brands'.

- Consumer online chatter is a crystal ball, an R&D lab and a sounding board.

- Consumers' mobile phones are their lifelines.

- Consumers trust bloggers as the new tastemakers and truth tellers.

PART I

The Future of Brands is Open

01:

Just for Openers

If you're still clinging to the comforts of the brand-made world, maybe you didn't get the memo (or the IM...or the text message) about the web-made world. The web-made world is created by individuals, not manufactured for the masses. And it's turned the brand-made world on its ear. Brands can't control this consumer-created space; they can only visit. That is, unless they engage richly, deeply and meaningfully with these new consumers who are stealing the show.

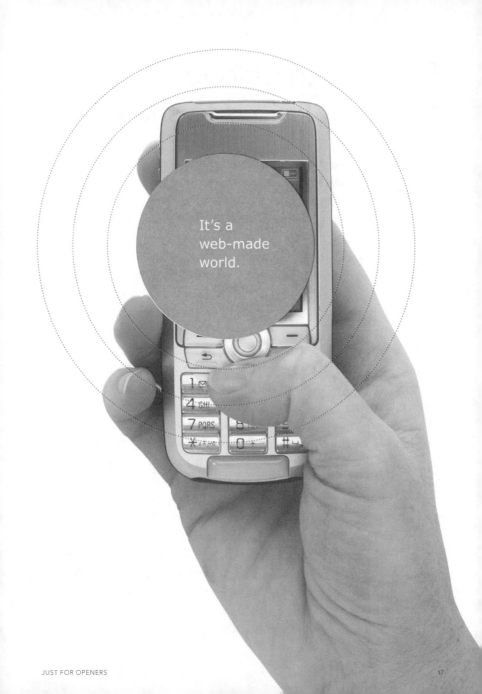

It's a
web-made
world.

To buy is to belong... and to belong is to share.

Some features of a great brand will never change. These include holistic, distinctive design. Carefully packaged messaging—and carefully messaged packaging. Innovative products that anticipate the needs of a changing audience. And brand experiences that have lasting emotional resonance with consumers.

The best brands also propagate a lifestyle. They are passports to a social realm beyond the individual drive to own and consume, where belonging becomes more important than buying. They are codes that communicate commonality and create a sense of community.

The iPod buyer is purchasing not only a portable music gadget, but also a backstage pass to a hip urban scene populated by Bono, The Black Eyed Peas and those übercool silhouetted dancers from the Apple ads.

An Abercrombie tee might look like just another shirt to the uninitiated, but to its wearers, it implies membership in a seemingly elite class of sexed-up power prepsters. Likewise, Harley-Davidson bikers aren't two-wheeling because it's the best transportation option; they're hitting the open road with other mavericks who live to ride and ride to live—together.

Though the most successful brands are those that foster a sense of distinctive community around their products, for today's consumers, community-by-brand-association is not enough. Now, before, during and after a purchase, consumers are engaging directly with each other through blogs, ratings and reviews, tagging and other interactive forums. They're sharing opinions, riffing off of each other's creativity and seizing control of the messages and values that brands once generated and propagated.

These peer-to-peer digital communications have begun to upstage brands as the gateway to coveted membership in communities—however abstract or ephemeral. For brands to survive this relationship shift, this digital displacement, they need to engage the tribal tendencies of online consumers on their own turf. Brands have to support those communities that have the closest affinity to them—and create some of their own.

Why are so many brands slow to react to this dramatic upsurge of consumer communities? Why are some brands seemingly closed to a two-way dialogue between themselves and the consumer? Or between one brand fan and another?

They're victims of their own success, for starters.

"The internet is the world's best platform for connecting people."

—**TIM ARMSTRONG**, PRESIDENT,
ADVERTISING AND COMMERCE, GOOGLE

THE CLOSED BRAND'S
DISTINGUISHED RUN

For the last thirty years or so, brilliantly controlled brand management was the perfect approach for persuading a mass market of credulous consumers, who willingly—even eagerly—put their faith in brands.

This has been the successful brand's time-tested formula: careful control over its image, meticulous attention to detail in execution, and a well-choreographed consumer experience at every touchpoint, all at the direction and discretion of the brand manager.

This tightly closed approach has helped mega brands like Coca-Cola, Microsoft, IBM, Disney, McDonald's, Nike and Starbucks dominate Interbrand's global Brand Scoreboard year after year.

While some of today's top brands continue to succeed by staying their current marketing course—sealed off from rising consumer influence in their hermetic universes—it's only a matter of time before chinks of cultural obsolescence appear in their armor. These will make brands vulnerable to waves of pressure not just from creative and communally-minded consumers but from nimble, risk-taking competitors as well. Against so many change agents, even the behemoth brands of the last and current century won't be able to stage a defense.

The closed brand will be overwhelmed by the passionate, powerful consumer who wants her brands open—or not at all.

WORLDVIEW OF A CLOSED BRAND	WORLDVIEW OF AN OPEN BRAND
TARGETS CONSUMERS	FOSTERS COMMUNITIES OF CONSUMERS
MONOLOGUE	DIALOGUE
AWARENESS	ENGAGEMENT
PUSH	PULL
EDITED ASSORTMENT	EVALUATED ASSORTMENT
FACE-TO-FACE CUSTOMER SERVICE	EFFICIENT SELF-SERVICE
SCRIPTED COMMUNICATION	TRANSPARENT COMMUNICATION
REQUESTED, PERIODIC FEEDBACK	24/7 FEEDBACK, INPUT-FOCUSED
CREATED BY MARKETERS	CO-CREATED WITH CONSUMERS
BRAND MANAGEMENT	BRAND STEWARDSHIP

Burton Blazes a Trail

While other brands might view interacting with virtual communities as risky, Jake Burton, founder and CEO of Burton Snowboards (not to mention founding father of the sport itself), recognized early on that his following was tech-savvy riders who were as active online as they were on the slopes.

Famous for chatting up fellow riders, Burton would solicit live feedback on every lift ride and cycle it back into web-based communications that nurtured valuable, transparent relationships with his customers. This allowed him to stay connected and approachable in the eyes of his customers even while he was scaling his business.

In 1997—a decade before it was a mainstream concept—Burton Snowboards launched an online initiative to enable customers to upload and share photos and en-gage in threaded discussions, which Burton's pro riders would join from time to time. Logging on to find postings from Burton pro riders was a rush for the amateur riders and a powerful credibility booster for the brand. This dialogue also provided first-hand data from avid riders, such as how often they took to the slopes, where they rode and their favorite styles. Burton was able to rapidly fold this information into new product development.

Jake Burton demonstrated old-school marketing savvy in knowing his customers well. And he showed he had early open branding chops by diving into his online community to build his brand and business. The result: he currently owns a marketshare that tops 35 percent.

RI CLIENT, 1994–2000

BRANDS AT RISK

Brands are at risk of losing cultural relevance in the web-made world because they're adopting trendy technologies without developing fresh insights into this new breed of interactive consumer. Even worse, some brands are simply waiting for this open season to pass, or at least to seem less chaotic, less of a threat to the completely choreographed success they've long enjoyed. Confronting accelerated change and the lack of appropriate resources to keep pace, marketers' resistance to the brave new world is understandable.

But the newly leveled marketplace described by Thomas Friedman in *The World is Flat: A Brief History of the Twentieth Century* needs a connect and collaborate brand communications model, not the old, vertical command and control one whose ultimate expression was the 30-second TV spot. The real risk for brands today is in not opening.

The bar is being raised by innovators like YouTube, Flickr, MySpace and Digg, which are redefining cultural relevance, paving the way for brand co-creation, social networking, citizen journalism and more. Now all brands are expected to provide faster and more customizable experiences, more enhanced content, and more opportunities for consumers to exchange ideas and be both seen and heard.

LEARNING TO LET GO

The open brand is an avid advocate of consumer participation—of leveraging the power of communities and networks—and enables the consumer to influence the brand and co-create its future.

The open brand seeks often unpredictable progress over carefully controlled perfection, cultivates and assimilates consumers' unorthodox opinions or creative ideas, and makes permanent room for consumers and their communities in the decision circle.

The successful open brand will operate under a new set of assumptions, including that the consumer will gladly ask for what she wants, engage in an ongoing dialogue and frequently share her opinions about brands with the online public. And that the brand must engage the consumer through transparent communication, trust the consumer to co-create the brand message and learn to be guided by impassioned amateurs.

Branding can no longer operate from the top down but instead must build from the bottom up, using as its platform the over one billion internet users accessing over 100 million web sites. Businesses that ignore consumer-opened branding do so at their own peril. It is an unstoppable movement acknowledged by no less than A.G. Lafley, CEO of Procter & Gamble, the largest mass marketer of our times. Lafley challenges: "Consumers are beginning in a very real sense to own our brands and participate in their creation. We need to learn to begin to let go."

Five Reasons to Open Your Brand

REVENUE

Gain access to larger, more diverse audiences more quickly, which will drive growth.

ROI

Spend marketing and advertising dollars more effectively and reduce mass media costs.

R&D

Collect innovative ideas from consumers and get an early pulse on new products to reduce inventory risk.

RELEVANCE

Keep pace in the digital age by showing cultural alignment with the rising expectations of demanding, participatory consumers.

RELATIONSHIPS

Turn your key assets—your consumers—into your best allies.

and the icing on the cake...

RECRUITING

Attract talent whose open source philosophy correlates with the tenets of an open brand.

02:

O.P.E.N.
for Business

In a web-made world, "open for business" doesn't mean what it once did. In fact, it now means "never closed." But in updating the sign that adorned storefronts for generations—to make it truly a sign of the times, it would have to read O.P.E.N....

THE FUTURE OF BRANDS IS OPEN

O...IS FOR ON-DEMAND.

Whatever today's consumers are seeking, they want it—and often get it—"right now." In a world where instant gratification is a way of life, on-demand is consumerism taken to its logical extreme. Overwhelmed by choice online and off, time-starved consumers demand accessibility, immediacy and findability. Of course, being an on-demand brand isn't easy: the logistics, infrastructure and resources needed are infinitely complex and costly, from just-in-time inventory systems to in-store pickup services to rapid information delivery to mobile commerce. But brands can no longer opt out of being on-demand if they want to capture the hearts and wallets of today's quicksilver consumers.

THE FUTURE OF BRANDS IS OPEN

P...IS FOR IS FOR PERSONAL.

Just as it was before the web proved itself a serious channel for brand-building and sales, the online landscape remains the province of the people, not companies. People online leave behind traces of their unique personalities, preferences and behaviors, both through passive clicking and surfing, and active participation and sharing. These vast realms of identifiable, unique individuals negate the old idea of target markets broadly bucketed by age, gender, income or education level. That's why, to be open, a brand must get personal— not with one market of many but with many markets of one—building relationships through constant consumer dialogue and effective cross-channel profile management that bring the brand closer to each consumer's real-time needs, wants and expectations.

THE FUTURE OF BRANDS IS OPEN

E...IS FOR ENGAGING.

Brands once competed for consumers' mindshare by pushing out mass market messaging they thought would appeal to their audience. Now, that audience has taken the stage, and brands must share the spotlight with creative consumers whose long tail of personal narrative, niche expertise, and mixed media productions can make a standard TV spot look static and self-absorbed. Marketers must develop content that is immersive, participatory and relevant in order to earn a place in the social web and consumer conversations. Interactivity is key to deepening consumers' emotional connection with a brand, so open brands must provide meaningful and engrossing experiences that foster consumer relationships online—and off.

N...IS FOR NETWORKED.

A single consumer has exponential brand potential when she goes online. She has a lifetime value, as she always has, but she also has viral value as she engages with her various online communities, as both the message and the medium. Open brands become part of social networks by marketing to the niche of communal consumers who interact with other like-minded consumers online. Though niche marketing is hardly new, the network effect of online word-of-mouth marketing is. So the more the brand works the network, the more the network works for the brand.

INTERNET AS CHIEF OPENING OFFICER

The good news is that companies don't have to hire yet another chief to get O.P.E.N. The internet is already working on your new strategic imperatives, though maximizing its potential might call for a business realignment. Brands need to move the digital channel toward their internal center of gravity, where it can radiate out to integrate and improve all consumer touchpoints.

A well-designed web site with interactive content can invite more consumer dialogue. Online promotions can drive foot traffic and increase offline sales. Web sites with visualization tools can provide in-depth decision support. Targeted online advertising and microsites can extend the reach, experience and impact of broadcast, print and out of home (OOH) advertising. E-catalogs and e-coupons can reduce analog costs of distribution. Mobile campaigns can deepen a brand relationship fueled by the web. Self-explanatory, easily navigable web sites can offset call center costs. And so on, as benefits emanate outward from the digital hub to every channel and every consumer.

The internet as chief opening officer doesn't need a corner office but it does need a central location within the enterprise to integrate otherwise disjointed business processes, customer marketing and operations. Once the internet becomes a brand's hub of interaction, consumers gain the fluid, responsive and expansive brand experience they crave. And you don't even have to pay an annual bonus.

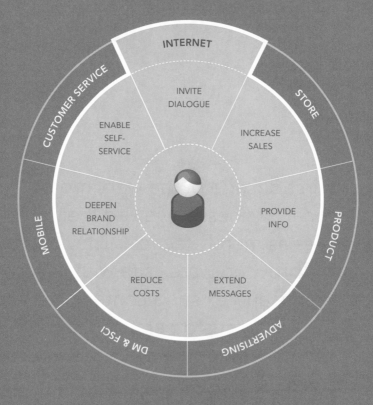

INTERNET

CUSTOMER SERVICE

STORE

MOBILE

PRODUCT

DM & FSCI

ADVERTISING

INVITE DIALOGUE

INCREASE SALES

ENABLE SELF-SERVICE

DEEPEN BRAND RELATIONSHIP

PROVIDE INFO

REDUCE COSTS

EXTEND MESSAGES

The internet is a platform that integrates all customer touchpoints, elevating the entire customer experience. Forrester Research predicts that over $1 trillion in offline sales will be web-influenced by 2012.

03:

Web 2.0 and the Alpha Openers

In the first decade of the web, most traditional businesses viewed their online initiatives as merely tactical. They created a basic "brochureware" site with linked documents and existing content, blasted a few emails to customers, and, if they were a bit ahead of the curve, advertised online with display ads and search engine keywords. Eyeballs, not consumer engagement, were marketers' endgame.

Sound familiar?

That was the Web 1.0, a simple term describing the digital dimension of a push marketing era that's currently giving way to the more dynamic, pull marketing-focused Web 2.0. Web 2.0 is a real sea change, not just a clever marketing moniker used to peg media stories, promote trade conferences and excite investors. It marks the arrival of fast-loading, media-rich, feed-driven sites that are virally communal, Application Programming Interface (API)-enabled, cross-platform-built, and disseminated across multiple channels and devices.

In simpler terms, Web 2.0 is home to the explosive world of blogs, user-generated content and social networking. Think of it as a new layer of the web that's user-controlled, spontaneous and instantly gratifying. Think of it as ground zero for the open brand.

The companies driving Web 2.0 are creating a media ecosystem that supports new online lifestyles and consumer experiences enjoyed daily by millions of users from every walk of life.

INNOVATIONS DRIVING THE NEXT REV OF THE WEB*

WEB 1.0	WEB 2.0
TOP-DOWN	BOTTOM-UP
OWNING	SHARING
READING	WRITING
HOME PAGES	BLOGS
PORTALS	RSS
TAXONOMY	TAGS
WIRES	WIRELESS
DIAL-UP	BROADBAND
HTML	RIA
WEB FORMS	WEB APPLICATIONS

*Adapted from Tim O'Reilly

With Web 2.0, the online population doesn't just read or watch content anymore: we also create our own. And we react energetically to what others have created. We don't have to venture out to multiple portals when we can use Really Simple Syndication (RSS) feeds to have self-selected content automatically delivered to our personal pages and devices, on our terms.

Consumers are no longer forced to follow the rigid taxonomy defined by information architects and database designers: we can tag content and pages for easy reference and navigation based on what we want to do—not on what others want us to do.

When we go online, we expect more than static, linear HTML pages, craving instead the smart and relevant Rich Internet Applications (RIAs) that now fulfill our digital desires with engaging interactive media.

And those tediously long web forms that required us to key in our personal minutiae and preferences again and again? They're being replaced by web applications that respond dynamically to each entry, practically reading our minds by filling in the blanks so that every step becomes increasingly efficient. And these apps remember us (yes, cookies can be our friend!), so they keep on helping us every time we log on.

Web 2.0 has also set us free in other ways. We're no longer tethered to our plug-based desktop computers; we're fully wireless and mobile, with laptops, PDAs, smart phones and Bluetooth devices. We've become intolerant of slow internet dial-ups, enjoying lightning-fast broadband or wireless at work and, increasingly, at home, where we network our households for multiple systems (including computers, entertainment centers and communications appliances). Technological convergence is converging upon us everywhere we turn, and we can't get enough of it.

THE ALPHA OPENERS

The companies that have brought all of this into our lives—these alpha openers, these enablers—just who are they?

They weren't necessarily the first to the party. Nor are they always the biggest kids on the block. They're the companies that have innovated or leveraged internet and telecommunications technologies to benefit consumers in new and significant ways.

The list includes the digital economy marquee names you expect—Google, MySpace, eBay, YouTube, Amazon, Wikipedia, Flickr and Linux—and some making smaller headlines, including del.icio.us, Bebo, Digg, Vox, Typepad and Technorati.

But the list isn't about defining a comprehensive "who's who" or hierarchy of digital achievers, so much as it is about locating the multiple epicenters of the vast cultural earthquake that's underway. These companies are the innovators and openers of the collective, creative and collaborative Web 2.0 experience.

ALPHA OPENERS

	OPENING INNOVATIONS
Linux	Open source
Amazon, eBay	Ratings and reviews
del.icio.us, Flickr	Social bookmarking and tagging
Flickr	Photo management
Wikipedia	Wiki
MySpace, Facebook, Bebo, Orkut, LinkedIn	Social networking
Typepad, Vox, Blogspot, Technorati, Blogger	Blogging tools, search and rankings
YouTube	Video sharing
Digg	Citizen journalism
Second Life	Virtual world
Google Maps	Mashups

ENABLING...	LESSONS FOR OPEN BRANDING
Collective volunteer efforts of programmers eager to improve software code for the greater good (and for fun).	The capacity and potential for shared goodwill and volunteerism is enormous; crowdsourcing is the new offshoring (without the cost).
Creating, sharing and searching for consumer opinions on everything from books to electronics.	Consumers are the new experts and tastemakers — and they rely on each other to make buying decisions.
Categorization and sharing of pages, images and other forms of content.	Organic organization is as viable as formal taxonomies.
Photos to be tagged, stored, searched and shared.	Web and mobile devices are portals for personal, shareable image archives.
One-click "edit this page" feature responsible for voluminous and rapid publishing of user-created content.	Making a contribution should be fast, easy and visible. And almost anyone should be allowed to do it.
Self-expression and socializing with unprecedented scale and speed.	People want reasons and avenues to connect with others, and experience a sense of belonging in these online communities.
Self-publishing, reader interaction and fast access to hot blogosphere topics.	Everyone's an aspiring pundit; get to know the most influential.
Easy access to online videos, delivering over 100 million video views per day with 65,000 new videos uploaded by consumers and businesses daily.	Amateurs can often be the most entertaining; the internet is a multimedia force.
Consumers as contributors and editors; winning content receives top billing.	Consumers can make their own news, and want a say in what soars or sinks.
An imaginary world with (mainly) user-generated avatars, relationships and events.	Consumers' capacity to imagine and play out personal fantasies is boundless.
Combinations of multiple content sources to create relevant new experiences.	Virtually anything can be combined for fun or utility.

THE OPEN BRAND'S CONSUMER ENGINE:
CREATING, SHARING AND INFLUENCING

While all eleven opening innovations are significant, it's their intermingling that has spawned three revolutionary and related online behaviors. Born of a multitude of online experiences, these behaviors—basic, universal human behaviors now augmented by the digital channel—have altered the brand playing field forever:

CREATING   The ability to make content in the form of words, pictures or video

SHARING   The ability to share content, ideas and opinions for the world to witness

INFLUENCING   The ability to affect other people's attitudes and actions

So, how do these behaviors impact average online consumers? When they interact with "everyday" brands such as Google, Amazon, Netflix and TiVo, they transfer their expectations and experiences to other brands with which they do business—with little regard or forgiveness for sector or category. If one brand doesn't give them the same kind of rich, interactive experience they've gotten from another, then the "lesser" brand is found lacking by comparison.

We're becoming so well-trained by the easy, intuitive tools that let us comparison shop while reading product reviews that we now become impatient when we can't see what other people think about a pair of shoes, a rental property or a recipe. And we're easily frustrated if we can't find online the warranty or care instructions for a product we've already purchased.

When our favorites aren't archived or shareable with friends, or when a photo or article we love or want to save can't be viewed on all of our devices, we're inconvenienced. We gradually and simply lose interest in the brands that aren't delivering services comparable to those that alpha opener brands offer.

The alpha openers have taught us that Web 2.0 and the branding frontier being blazed across it is about much more than media-hyped, user-created content.

Web 2.0 is about using the internet less as a tool for linking pages and more as a dynamic, global operating system—a virtual nervous system for communicating and conducting business in a real-time, distributed fashion. It's about engaging consumers wherever their digital passions lie, from software code tinkering or

> "The web as interaction between people is really
> what the web is. That was what it was designed to be,
> a collaborative space where people can interact."
>
> —TIM BERNERS-LEE, CO-FOUNDER, WORLD WIDE WEB

creating ratings and reviews to living in virtual worlds or mashing up multiple content sources. It's ultimately about using technology to enable, expand and catalyze marketing mixes that only get better with more cooks in the kitchen.

To talk the Web 2.0 talk before you walk the walk, consider these questions:

- How many of the alpha openers' lessons have you applied to your business?
- To what extent is your web site fast-loading, media-rich and feed-driven?
- Are you supporting consumers' chief Web 2.0 behaviors— creating, sharing and influencing?
- Are your brand marketers tech savvy? Can they communicate and collaborate effectively with IT?
- Do you understand the motivations of the online population?

OPEN TO MORE?

PART II

The Rise of the iCitizen

04:

Consumerism's Counterpoint

The simple acts of shopping, buying and selling will never be the same. Profoundly reshaping them are online social and cultural activities that seem far removed from consumerism's siren call—archiving photos, social networking, blogging, bookmarking, swarming, IMing, twittering, video scraping, mashing up. But savvy marketers know better.

Digital rituals both mundane and exotic help form individuals' and groups' social identities, and along with them people's tastes, preferences, values—what's important to know, what to buy in order to belong (or be unique), what to share with or recommend to friends and family.

Moreover, many of these digital pastimes are no longer "early adopter" behaviors limited to a minority of tech hipsters. Web audience measurement firm Hitwise reports that social media usage—a potent mix of creating, sharing and influencing—grew a staggering 668 percent from April 2005 to April 2007. According to a 2006 Pew Internet & American Life Project report, 35 percent of American adult internet users are generating content—everything from posting photographs to contributing prose to web sites. More than seventy million blogs and growing fast, and over 65,000 videos uploaded daily to YouTube (not to mention the over one hundred million videos watched daily) are an outpouring of amateur production and self-serve entertainment that no marketer can afford to ignore.

Despite these statistics, there are skeptics about the importance of social networking and consumers' content creation to brands. They believe that marketing to these behaviors—tapping them as new sources of sway and of storytelling, respectively, for the brand—still means catering to too few people. And they point to the minority of actual content creators on sites heavily reliant

"…Individuals are changing the nature of the information age…the creators and consumers of content are transforming art, politics and commerce—they are engaged citizens of a new digital democracy."
—**RICHARD STENGEL**, MANAGING EDITOR, *TIME MAGAZINE*, DECEMBER 25, 2006

upon CGM—such as YouTube, Flickr, Digg, Gather and Wikipedia. Usability consultant and author Jakob Nielsen wrote in 2006 that, "In most online communities, 90 percent of users are lurkers who never contribute, nine percent of users contribute a little, and one percent of users account for almost all the action."

The problem with this 1/9/90 argument—or, in the more common formulation, the 20/80 rule (20 percent of causes deliver 80 percent of consequences)—is two-fold. First, most brand web sites are not wholly dependent upon content creation per se in order to thrive. An e-commerce site might feature a CGM campaign or consumer ratings and reviews on the home page, or might be part of a social shopping network, but these are complementary to the e-commerce priority. Second, there are three social web behaviors (hence, a larger portion of the online population) that can drive business: creating, sharing and influencing, not just content creation alone. The iProspect Social Networking User Behavior Study (by JupiterResearch and Ipsos-Insight, April 2007) shows how the three behaviors work in concert: it found that one out of three internet users "is already taking advantage of a site containing user-generated content to help make a decision to buy, or not to buy something."

Animating discussions of the social web's early adopter or content-creating minorities is the debate over influence: who or what has it and how it happens online. Proponents of "the law of the few," a principle Malcolm Gladwell popularized in his book, *The Tipping Point*, place their bet on online charismatic individuals with certain personality traits that, in the right combination of roles, can start a social (or consumer) "epidemic." Opponents of the law of the (vital) few argue that the online social network is far more important than a minority of so-called influentials, hence, marketing to the majority is the new imperative. A CNET

> *"Companies need to acknowledge different levels of creativity exist and offer relevant online experience to facilitate people's expression of creativity at all levels. This means leading, guiding and providing scaffolds as well as clean slates to encourage people at all levels of creativity. Recognize and reward people for the co-creative efforts, but keep in mind that intrinsic motivation beats extrinsic motivation."*
> —**LIZ SANDERS, Ph. D.**, FOUNDER, MAKETOOLS, LLC

Research study supports the majority argument; it shows that a full 85–90 percent of online consumers acquire enough digital savvy—through searching, surfing, reading reviews, etc.—to become reliable "experts" to friends and family. The information they share, even within their relatively small spheres of influence, can significantly influence purchase behavior.

What is beyond debate is this: the digital behaviors of creating, sharing and influencing have altered consumers' expectations of brands. Consumers now expect to be involved in the creation and promotion of goods and services. After all, they're creating and sharing their own valuable products hourly: blog content, homegrown videos, social profiles—and even building their own small businesses and personal brands in the process. Gartner estimates 80 percent of internet users will have their own avatars by 2011. Consumers consequently want to feel engaged in the commercial world's creative processes rather than simply being the focus of their output.

The Resource Interactive 2007 iCitizen Motivational Study showed that 86% of the U.S. online population or roughly 200 million people (Internet Usage and World Population Statistics for June 30, 2007) are creating, sharing and influencing. Among those that have not adopted these behaviors, 21 percent would "like a

The iCitizen's Prosuming Predecessors

Futurist Alvin Toffler coined the term "prosumer" in his 1980 bestseller, *The Third Wave*. A hybrid of "producer" and "consumer," the prosumer dates to preindustrial, pre-currency times (the first socio-economic wave), when people produced what they consumed out of necessity. Toffler believed the standardized products of mass production (characterizing the Second Wave) would eventually lead to a desire for post-industrial customization (the Third Wave), which meant consumers would once again become involved in production.

The web-made world is more about digital customization—and mass collaboration—than the kind of mass customization of real-world consumer goods Toffler envisioned. Still, Toffler's is an appropriate model for the icitizenry. Consumers-turned-producers are also amateurs turned—or turning—pro, shaping and sharing the assets of our knowledge economy: ideas.

The psychological profile of icitizens has everything to do with their ideas, their production. First, they possess *expertise*—knowledge of and devotion to a subject that, however narrow or quirky, becomes a part of the ideation value chain when distributed through the internet's social networks. In the process, it challenges traditional authority (the mass media, church, state, university, medical profession, parents, etc.).

Second, icitizens have an abiding and contagious *passion* about their expertise. Their energy and enthusiasm—in abundance and summoned after work, on the weekends, in the wee hours—to create avatars or write code or review a vacation spot took the offline world by surprise.

Finally, there is *transparency*—a guileless, honest willingness to share personal desires, dreams and perspectives without professional filters or the subterfuge of a spin machine. The direct, unmediated peer-to-peer nature of the social web also makes transparency nearly an inalienable right of its icitizens.

*"YouTube scooped the 2006 Victoria's Secret Fashion Show by airing
it before national TV did. But YouTube had only some of the
content and none of the production quality. Really, it's the way
of the world today, isn't it? You can't prepare for some of this stuff.
All you can do is commit to a constant exploration of new sources,
and be open to change when it comes. Because it will."*

—**ED RAZEK**, CHIEF MARKETING OFFICER, LIMITED BRANDS

brand/company more" if simply asked to participate.

We call these conspicuously creative and involved consumers "icitizens," in part because the word "citizen" is back in vogue, attached to "journalism" or "marketers" or other phenomena associated with the social web's participatory ethos.

To capitalize on the icitizenry's thriving culture and their collective desire to be part of brands' value creation, marketers have to zero in on their motivations for doing all that they do. Traditional consumer segments or personas will have to be updated for this uniquely complex digital population, one that prompted *TIME Magazine* in 2006 to name "You" as their "Person of the Year" for doing nothing less than "…seizing the reins of the global media, for founding and framing the new digital democracy, for working for nothing and beating the pros at their own game."

A MOTIVATIONAL MASHUP

The motivations of the icitizenry consist of competence, collectivism, cultural change and celebrity. According to The Resource Interactive 2007 iCitizen Motivational Study, the first motivation, belonging to a full 74 percent of icitizens (148 million), is to acquire digital competence: to use the web and its proliferating array of tools (from blog software to multimedia widgets) to achieve certain goals, whether they be musical expression or in-the-know shopping or simply having fun. The mindset of icitizens driven by this basic motivation is simply "I CAN"—a seemingly modest motivation to keep pace in the web-made world. But make no mistake: the marketer that appeals directly to this drive for digital proficiency must package sophisticated DIY tools in an easy-to-use branded experience—no mean feat. Consider the relatively anonymous tagging enthusiast "Rtwendel21," who exemplifies the motivation to be digitally competent. Having mastered tagging on del.icio.us, this social bookmarker now potentially influences millions of others searching for similar subjects online. A brand interested in capturing the competence-minded icitizen might, in this instance, add social bookmarking options to its site.

Sixteen percent of icitizens—32 million—are motivated by online or mobile socializing, particularly with others who share their passions and interests. Of that sixteen percent, fifty percent are digital millennials. This group's mindset is best summed up as "I CONNECT." To leverage this spirit of collectivism, open brand marketers must address groups, not just individuals, by supporting and nurturing their shared enthusiasms. Markos "Kos" Moulitsas Zúniga exemplifies this motivation. The left-leaning political blogger whose dailykos.com frequently tops Technorati's blog rankings has created arguably one of the most vital (yet virtual) meeting grounds for the Democratic party.

Seven percent of icitizens—14 million—seek to effect (generally good) change on behalf of others. The mindset here is "I AM"— the embodiment of an idea, a brand, a lifestyle, a movement. These change agents can accrue tremendous credibility, making them valuable to marketers seeking reliable and charismatic spokespersons or sponsorship platforms. Top-selling eBay trainer, spokesperson and author Marsha Collier, whose eBay books, including *eBay for Dummies* (1999), have sold over one million copies, is not an eBay employee but is nevertheless one of the brand's most important evangelists. Collier has helped make eBay an exciting pastime, a source of supplemental income and an emblem of achievable entrepreneurialism to millions worldwide.

The motivation to achieve celebrity or heightened influence within their group, whatever the size, drives three percent of icitizens—about six million. The mindset among these icitizens is "I MATTER"—to a community of followers, to the mainstream media, even in a personal way to a brand. These fame-seeking icitizens can be a ready-made asset for open brands because many such icitizens become brands in their own right, inhabiting a universe rich with social currency. Web-catapulted comedian Dane Cook's personal brand has spawned legions of fans who've made him the highest *Billboard*-charting funnyman in 29 years.

> *Tools and web sites that encourage consumer participation have been around since the start of the web but they've experienced a recent spike in popularity. With new tools, experiences and the fun aspects of the emerging social web, there's a resulting broader appeal and broader access to information. The key is the information's credibility, which is easily validated; the more credible it is, the greater the consumer's adoption of new tools and technologies tied to that information.*
>
> —**PATTI FREEMAN EVANS**, SENIOR ANALYST, RETAIL INDUSTRY, JUPITERRESEARCH

THE ICITIZENRY'S MOTIVATIONS

A map of what drives the online population of makers and doers, movers and shakers, and how to leverage their influence.

74%   16%

COMPETENCE

"I CAN"
Use web tools for fun,
learning and efficiency

COLLECTIVISM

"I CONNECT"
Connect and share
with people who have
similar interests

EVERYDAY

STRENGTH OF CLOSE TIES

- Expert majority
- Friends and family
- Increase trial and conversion

EVERYDAY icitizens, though greater in number, have less social clout than do ELITE icitizens. But theoretically, anyone can "ascend" the ranks of the icitizenry when their notoriety is coupled with network effects.

7%

3%

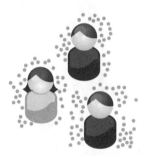

CULTURAL CHANGE
"I AM"
Effect change that improves companies, products or the experience of others

CELEBRITY
"I MATTER"
Seek recognition or some degree of fame

ELITE →

STRENGTH OF WEAK TIES
- Vital few
- Vast networks
- Build awareness and equity

05:

The Power of One. Gazillion.

A potential star is born in every blog, and, as the new saying goes, social profiles make people famous to at least fifteen people (instead of, as Andy Warhol quipped, famous for fifteen minutes). If celebrity isn't quite what it once was, it's certainly bigger as a trend. Momentous, even. In this era of self-made multimedia mavens, the number of virtual world stars has exploded, even as the medium for their fame has shrunk to the size of a laptop or iPhone.

And it's not just online: in a world where a talented nobody can rise to the top on *American Idol*, the masses are empowered as never before to generate, celebrate and venerate their crowd-made stars.

Such homegrown fame—especially among web celebs—has even nipped at the cultural clout of the ultimate tracker of innovative tech culture, *Wired*. According to Chris Anderson, the magazine's editor-in-chief and author of *The Long Tail*, the competitive threat of the icitizenry—which is wagged by its own long tail of celebrity—is very real. Addressing the Resource Interactive iCitizen Symposium (2006), he said, "*Wired* isn't losing to any single blog. Instead, we're losing readers to an army of blogs with very narrow niches. Micro niches. Nano niches. Too many to count."

When elite icitizens' singular insights or talents are coupled with network effects, their web celeb status frequently evolves to the big time of larger screens and lucrative deals, whether sought or not. So, their popularity grows exponentially, with the web as both platform and catalyst.

To use a familiar metaphor, all icitizens are uniquely passionate and transparent about their expertise but some of these snowflakes soon snowball into larger-than-life personalities. Their notoriety achieves critical mass, and their influence gains momentum and reach in a way that is particular to the web.

Marketers at this point should conduct research to identify the icitizens and spheres of influence most valuable to them. Everyday icitizens, with smaller social networks, are ideally positioned to help marketers tap "the strength of close ties"—those between the everyday icitizen and her friends and family. What sociologist Mark Granovetter called "the strength of weak ties" belongs to the elite icitizens, whose more widespread influence reaches people not known to the cultural change-motivated or celebrity-seeking icitizen. Because of the trust and familiarity existing between everyday icitizens and their closer-knit networks, they are best leveraged for driving trial and purchase. Elite icitizens can be used to build broad awareness of a brand. Indeed, they might be positioned as the next face or voice of a brand. Online "auditions" and voting, coupled with studies of social media archetypes, can help identify an elite icitizen with plenty of network charisma and attributes highly compatible with the brand.

How strategic is your brand's relationship with the icitizenry?

 Do any of the icitizenry's main motivations (competence, collectivism, cultural change and celebrity) align with your consumer segments or consumer personas? If so, how are you marketing to this motivation?

 Have you identified your icitizen truth tellers and tastemakers? Are you mining the blogosphere for the most influential and charismatic among them?

 Do you know how and where your consumers interact with everyday and elite icitizens? Have you discovered their common traits, and learned how to capitalize on them?

 How are elite icitizens influencing your consumers' awareness of and opinions about your brand?

06:

Portraits of the iCitizen

Just who are these personal brands? These self-styled celebrities? Which one is a long tail tastemaker? A social networking sensation? A millennial Web 2.0 mogul? What marketers must know is the name, notoriety and network effect of elite icitizens potentially important to their brand, because they are a kind of name, rank and serial number for those who are populating the social web frontlines.

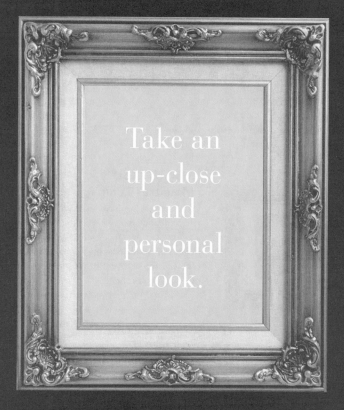

Take an
up-close
and
personal
look.

Our portrait gallery of icitizens only begins to show
just how widely brands must cast their nets to catch up
with these trendsetters, truth tellers and tastemakers.

Marsha Collier

NOTORIETY: Written over a dozen eBay books, including *eBay for Dummies*.

NETWORK EFFECT: eBay PowerSeller and the top-selling eBay author.

www.coolebaytools.com

WHO SHOULD CARE? eBay management, eBay enthusiasts, entrepreneurs, business schools, anyone looking to enter the eBay community and others…

Markos "Kos" Moulitsas Zúniga

NOTORIETY: Democratic blogger extraordinaire whose views, friends and online fundraising can swing elections.

NETWORK EFFECT: Receives between 14 and 24 million visits per month to his blog, and his YearlyKos is the very first political blogger convention.

www.dailykos.com

WHO SHOULD CARE? Print newspapers, Democratic and Republican parties, policy makers and wonks, political analysts and pundits, politics junkies and others…

Harriet Klausner

NOTORIETY: Posted more than 14,000 book reviews on amazon.com.

NETWORK EFFECT: Publishers send her 50 free books a week in hopes of attracting her attention and reviews.

http://thebestreviews.com/user5

WHO SHOULD CARE? Online bookstores, publishers, authors, avid readers and others…

Ashley Qualls

NOTORIETY: High schooler amassed a fortune as founder/CEO and webmaster of a social networking site specializing in profile layouts and graphics.

NETWORK EFFECT: Whateverlife.com attracts a larger audience than *Teen Vogue*, *Seventeen* and *CosmoGIRL* put together.

www.whateverlife.com

WHO SHOULD CARE? Rival social networking sites, teen marketers, educators and ethnographers, high schoolers, parents and others…

Frank Warren

NOTORIETY: Started online community art project based on secret confessions sent on postcards.

NETWORK EFFECT: His site won eight Bloggy awards, including Weblog of the Year, and has 4 million unique visitors a month; has become a not-so-secret book series success as well.

www.postsecret.blogspot.com

WHO SHOULD CARE? Memoir publishers, social scientists, non-profit public assistance programs, documentary filmmakers, true confessions fans, secret keepers and others….

Cory Doctorow

NOTORIETY: Gives his novels away for free online.

NETWORK EFFECT: More than 700,000 copies of his books have been downloaded.

www.craphound.com

WHO SHOULD CARE? Book retailers and publishers, avid fiction fans, screenwriters and TV writers, self-publishers and others…

Perez Hilton

NOTORIETY: Celebrity gossip blogger who inspires controversy with every post.

NETWORK EFFECT: Sparked over 7.1 million page views in one day when actress Lindsay Lohan was arrested.

www.perezhilton.com

WHO SHOULD CARE? Celebrity and lifestyle magazines, celebrity TV shows, entertainment properties, celebrity coaches, star-struck fans and others...

Stephanie Klein

NOTORIETY: Known as the blogosphere Carrie Bradshaw.

NETWORK EFFECT: Receives over 100,000 unique visitors per month to her blog; her posts and popularity led to her first book, *Straight Up and Dirty*.

www.stephanieklein.blogs.com

WHO SHOULD CARE? Lifestyle magazines, TV producers, therapists, straight shooters, femme fatales, lonely hearts and others...

Kamini

NOTORIETY: Recorded a hugely popular hip-hop song and video that aired on YouTube.

NETWORK EFFECT: Within two months of the YouTube video posting, signed a record deal with RCA.

www.kamini.fr/home.html

WHO SHOULD CARE? Music labels, youth fashion brands, musicians, hip-hop fans, YouTube hopefuls and others...

William Sledd

NOTORIETY: Star of "Ask a Gay Man" fashion series.

NETWORK EFFECT: Rookie fashion critic makes it into bastions of fashion *WWD*, *Elle* and *Glamour* thanks to YouTube and Facebook.

www.williamsledd.com and www.sleddhead.com

WHO SHOULD CARE? Fashion editors, fashion retailers and brands, TV producers, fashionistas, the style-challenged and others…

Ze Frank

NOTORIETY: Digital performance artist.

NETWORK EFFECT: Over 25,000 people watched his online show daily to laugh and learn about everything from dorky dance moves to net neutrality.

www.zefrank.com

WHO SHOULD CARE? Event marketers and planners, comedy venues, videographers, comedy fans and others…

Salam Pax

NOTORIETY: The "Baghdad Blogger" who reported on the invasion and war in Iraq.

NETWORK EFFECT: During the invasion of Baghdad and early days of the Iraq war, half of all page views on Blogger.com were for Pax's eyewitness reports of the unfolding conflict.

http://justzipit.blogspot.com/

WHO SHOULD CARE? U.S. military, news media, military families and supporters, concerned citizens and others…

Jonathan Schwartz

NOTORIETY: Sun Microsystems CEO is first Fortune 500 blogger.

NETWORK EFFECT: Thousands are embracing Schwartz's outreach as a caring, sharing corporate citizen.

www.blogs.sun.com/jonathan

WHO SHOULD CARE? Corporate CEOs, the software industry, high-minded high-tech job seekers, Silicon Valley do-gooders and others...

Geriatric1927

NOTORIETY: 80-year-old British storyteller who makes autobiographical YouTube videos.

NETWORK EFFECT: Since first video debuted in August 2006, his flicks have been viewed nearly 5 million times, and have garnered more than 44,000 subscribers.

http://www.youtube.com/profile?user=geriatric1927

WHO SHOULD CARE? UK tourism bureaus, advertisers targeting seniors, the AARP, hipsters young and old, and others...

Dane Cook

NOTORIETY: Web-catapulted comedian

NETWORK EFFECT: The highest *Billboard*-charting comedian in 29 years, *Saturday Night Live* host and film actor, he tours to sold-out performances (while still using the web as home base).

www.myspace.com/danecook

WHO SHOULD CARE? Comedy producers, live performance venues, youth marketers, aspiring entertainers, open mic fans, laugh lovers and others…

Jud Laipply

NOTORIETY: Best known for his viral "Evolution of Dance" clip.

NETWORK EFFECT: #1 Most Viewed All Time Video, #1 Top Favorites Video and #4 Most Discussed Video on YouTube.

www.theevolutionofdance.com

WHO SHOULD CARE? Corporate event planners, human resources consultants, pop culture fans, dancers (good and bad) and others...

Staff of *Harry Potter* fansite MuggleNet

NOTORIETY: Weekly podcast about Harry Potter's world.

NETWORK EFFECT: Won 2006 People's Choice Podcast Award. Some 50,000 *Harry Potter* fans from 183 countries listen in each week.

www.mugglecast.com and www.mugglenet.com

WHO SHOULD CARE? Book retailers, *Harry Potter* franchisees, youth marketers, *Harry Potter* fans, fantasy writers, budding wizards and others...

...and MILLIONS more...

07:

The Digital Millennials

NAME: The Digital Millennials

NOTORIETY: The most digitally connected generation in history.

NETWORK EFFECT: Over 82,000,000 of them are redefining—or will redefine— the rules of engagement for brands.

ALL BRAND MARKETERS SHOULD CARE

82

MILLION

You read that right—over 82 million of them.
So who are they?

The millennial generation grew up while technological convergence was making its way across giant industry sectors and small digital devices alike. Little wonder, then, that their lives blend the once-separate spheres of private and public, consumption and production, entertainment and education, community and creativity, shopping and self-actualization. The fabric of a millennial's life is woven from these threads, with technology as the loom that brings them seamlessly together.

What does a marketer need to know about the generation born between 1982 and 2000, a.k.a. echo boomers, Gen Y, the IM or bling generation? Plenty. They are a generation soon to be larger than the baby boomers and with unprecedented discretionary spending power. They possess a keen sense of self-entitlement and self-worth, and have high aspirations for the future. Nearly 40 percent believe they will earn over $100,000 per year by the time they reach 30, and nearly one-third of them believe—not feel or wish—that they will become famous, according to a 2006 MTV study. And over three-fourths of them believe that brands should routinely ask for their opinions.

In 2006, Resource Interactive conducted an in-depth study of "first wave" millennials, aged 14–24. Through video diaries and online focus groups, Resource mapped the millennials' daily digital interactions to examine their larger behavioral patterns and the values that motivate them.

Friendship is one of their most cherished values—and it drives much of their online networking behavior. Like boomers, most millennials have a small, close circle of three to five friends, and an extended network of 5–25 relatives, friends and colleagues. But millennials depart from older generations when it comes to their pecking order of device-dependent or digital friends, each linked to the technology that sustains (or even defines) their relationships.

Keep it real.
Being fake is worse than being uncool.

Hear me out.
I have ideas and want to make my mark.

Be original or don't be.
Get there first to win my attention.

My way…now.
I want it how I want it. Period.

Entertain me.
It's all about me—and my friends—give us a laugh.

"Best friends" might have never "fleshmet" in person—yet chat daily via IM, while classmates might rarely talk face-to-face—yet text or talk often via cell phone. It's the medium of the messenger that matters as much as the message itself for millennials.

For the diehard social networking enthusiasts, "friends" are made up of casts of thousands. These virtual friends are accumulated via profiles at MySpace and Facebook and others, where they can quickly connect with others who share their interests, and gain popularity (or the perception of it) through the "network effect" of fast-growing friend lists.

What does this digitized definition of friendship mean to marketers? It means that brands have to get inside millennials'

"I think that it's almost engrained in us. I think we wouldn't feel connected to the world if we didn't have AIM on our computer, if we couldn't log into MySpace."
—Emily, age 22

"My friend doesn't have a cell phone. I'm about to drop her because I never talk to her."
—Mickey, age 16

"I may not have much money, but I will influence more people than you can imagine, so if companies show me what I want, they'll be just fine."
—Matthew, age 21

"Of course I want to be famous. I want everyone to know who I am. I want everybody to know my background. I want everybody to know how amazing I could be if I tried. I've always dreamed of doing something that would make me extremely popular. I think I'm already famous at school."—Laura, age 15

"Most online ads are just flat out boring. I can train my eyes not to see them if I want. It's like when my mom talks sometimes, it's that same deal. Yea, yea, yea, but you don't hear a word she says."—Colin, age 18

network to win their attention. As with most of their decision-making, millennials act collaboratively and take the digital pulse of their peers before making a purchase—and increasingly, they do so throughout the entire purchase journey: witness the rise of social shopping. Consumers offer and seek advice—and get to know each other—on shopping cohort sites such as Shopstyle.com and Stylehive.com. Eventually, retailers will have to support online purchasers who desire the real-time, virtual presence of friends.

Brands are playing second fiddle as millennials turn to the new cultural authority: their vast and multilayered social networks that serve as their lifeline for support, dialogue and shared experiences. The brand communications that once initiated the consumer journey are increasingly ineffective for many reasons, including time-shifting and channel proliferation. But for millennials in particular, traditional brand communications are received as so much white noise to be vigilantly filtered. When brand messages break into the hot topic migrations of a social network, it is because they targeted a millennial cohort or consumer persona successfully, and were endorsed as "pass-along worthy." At this point, the network's many communities and clubs, alliances and dalliances, take over. Both weak and close ties in this setting can more effectively amplify a message or implicitly endorse a product than can a multimillion dollar mass marketing campaign that fails to connect with the right people—famous or otherwise.

08:

Trust is in the Network

With the power of social networking, infinite online searching and mobile connectedness, consumers now have access to a boisterous bazaar of public opinion. How much is this easy access to the opinions and insights of individuals altering consumers' perceptions of authority? Quite a bit. Their sense of who has authority and who deserves it has changed dramatically.

A 2006 Edelman Study revealed that trust in a "person like me" rose from 20 percent in 2003 to 68 percent in 2006—an increase of more than 300 percent.

If icitizens are turning to each other for news and views instead of relying on official and traditional sources—including brands themselves, it's not simply because of the exhilarating access to an unfiltered online community. The growth of trust in a peer network is tied to waning trust in traditional cultural authorities and institutions—the church and state, educators and, yes, brands and the mass media. Consumers are less trusting because they're jaded by everything from lackluster customer service and brand blandness to a wave of white-collar corruption in the form of the scandals of Enron, Worldcom, Adelphia, Tyco and even Martha Stewart.

As a result, icitizens have taken matters into their own hands. They've transformed themselves from passive receivers of information to active retrievers, creators and judges of it. They've become information DIYers. David Altman, Senior Vice President and General Manager of Bath & Body Works Direct, said, "Our customer is very tuned in to advice from her trusted friends and family, and though she's checking out magazines and shop-at-home channels, the trend is definitely peer-to-peer. She is interested in what other women like her have to say about beauty."

> *"To join a conversation or social network relevant to your brand, you first have to know and clearly understand who the advocates are in your target market. Advocates like to share positive things, in bigger circles, and are 44 percent more likely to post their opinions."*
> —**LORNA BORENSTEIN**, PRESIDENT, MOVE, INC., AND FORMER YAHOO! EXECUTIVE

> *"We know of five or six influential Gymboree-focused sites that moms have created themselves. We absolutely take note of the sites' content and comments because we know the perspectives are honest. We love that our customers are so passionate about our products that they want to talk about it. That's always terrific for the brand."*
>
> —**SUSAN NEAL**, VP BUSINESS DEVELOPMENT, GYMBOREE

PEOPLE LIKE ME

In contrast to the pre-internet world, a "person like me" no longer has to live in the same neighborhood, belong to the same book club, have kids at the same school or work at the same firm. In fact, a "person like me" doesn't have to be anything like "me"—at least, not demographically. That person just has to share a similar interest or experience, which I discover while surfing, searching or checking out my favorite social networking site. That "person like me" becomes an ally and advisor by virtue of having a seemingly independent, informed opinion about a subject that is relevant to me.

Forrester Research reports that over 52 percent of adult consumers typing queries into search engines are doing so to make or influence routine purchase decisions. All consumers are 50 percent more likely to be influenced by word-of-mouth recommendations from their peers than by radio or TV ads, according to a Nielsen BuzzMetrics 2005 report. Why? Because trust is now in the network—in groups of interconnected "people like me."

Acceptable Bias

The vast majority of online consumers simply want to make informed decisions and to do so, ironically, they go online to seek largely subjective perspectives from complete strangers. This seems like a contradiction: isn't objectivity consumers' Holy Grail? No, transparency is.

There's an inherent acceptance of bias in the perceived absence of vested interest. Everyone's got an opinion—in other words, a bias—but those opinions have more legitimacy if we believe they're based on personal experience or the desire to help others through sharing, rather than on the tactics of corporate persuasion. When a consumer wants more than brochure copy and an online price check of vacation packages, she goes to tripadvisor.com to get the "truth" before booking. What could be better than reading an entry from an inspired traveler "like me"—someone who prefers, say, a boutique hotel in a bustling arts neighborhood that's walking distance to shopping, museums and wine bars?

Those "biased" opinions acquire even greater legitimacy if they're grouped with other similar ones or constitute a rating system of popularity or reliability; eBay buyers' opinions about sellers are archived so that sellers' trustworthiness over time becomes a nearly objective certainty.

The trick to making acceptable bias work in a brand's favor is simple: enable and foster dialogue about your brand and products without seeming to influence, interfere with or manipulate it. Give icitizens a forum, a gathering place, a community of their own. If such places already exist for sharing product opinions and tips—and it's highly likely they do, tread lightly on their turf and identify your contributions. Finally, as does NYTimes.com/travel and others, organize your reviews by affinity groups, so it's easy for consumers to find the insights of others like themselves.

> *"Consumers will never tire of writing reviews and will only get more engaged in their brands and communities of choice."*
> —**BRETT A. HURT**, FOUNDER AND CEO, BAZAARVOICE

FROM MARKETING FUNNEL TO FISH

According to Forrester Research (2007), when it comes to trust, consumer-generated media consistently outranks professional sources. By now it's clear that consumer-generated media is not a geek fad or passing techno-fancy. "The number of people who create content…is expected to increase significantly as the user-generated content movement gathers steam….Globally, the number of user-generated content creators will reach 238 million in 2011, up from 137 million in 2007."

As word-of-mouth platforms grow and traditional marketing tools lose impact, the propensity of a customer base to recommend products and services to others will be regarded as a key measure of brand equity. Consequently, brands must rethink the customer journey to purchase, and allocate more resources for strengthening the peer connections and conversations along the way; these interactions are now the essential relay for an ad campaign or other marketing initiative.

Ad campaigns themselves can—and should— be more targeted in our ad-skeptical and ad-skipping times. Mobile, the antithesis of a mass medium, can make event, promotional and video marketing highly targeted to a person's real-time needs and interests. Embeddable media players or other types of widgets— the latest in pull marketing—once dropped by the consumer onto her web page can be a welcome advertising window, provided the content relates to areas of interest chosen by the consumer. If your brand generates new content frequently or a blogger's content or other news publisher is relevant to your brand, RSS feeds can likewise deliver ads along with consumer-chosen content right to their digital front doors.

After the targeted campaign or content raises awareness about and interest in a brand, marketers should focus on the "scenic route"—the social and increasingly circuitous paths their messages then take. Fine-tuning consumer relationship management programs keeps a brand in touch with and up to date about a consumer's wants and needs. Providing valuable digital CSI (creating, sharing, influencing) tools is the brand's ticket to go along for the icitizen ride through social networks and creative remixing. Hosting or sponsoring events pulls consumers toward the brand's human dimension.

All of this activity in the middle of the consumer journey fundamentally changes its shape, from the traditional funnel to a new school fish. The opening of the former funnel is now smaller—because it's more targeted—at the "mouth" (where brand communications via mass media have historically initiated the journey), largest around the "belly" because of consumer queries and activities, creative inventions and interventions. It then fans out at the end into a multidirectional "tail" of post-purchase behaviors that amplify consumer opinions and advocacy.

In light of this funnel-to-fish evolution, companies need to re-architect their brand communications to determine the most effective tactics for intriguing icitizens, engaging their peer network, and inspiring both to move through the purchase journey.

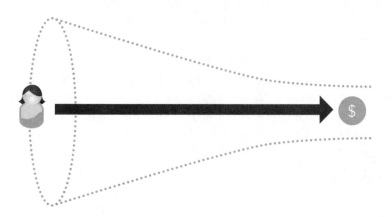

The impact of traditional brand communications at the outset of the consumer purchase journey is decreasing.

FROM FUNNEL TO FISH

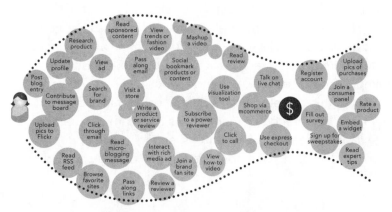

The prevalence and impact of consumer-driven activities, particularly online, change the shape of the journey.

A NEW CONSUMER JOURNEY

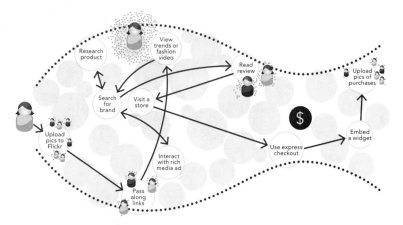

This is one of countless consumer journeys that are increasingly non-linear, multichannel, and dependent upon the creating, sharing, and influencing behaviors of icitizens.

THE ROLE OF THE BRAND

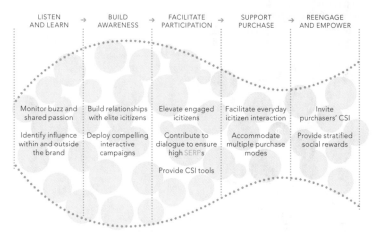

LISTEN AND LEARN	BUILD AWARENESS	FACILITATE PARTICIPATION	SUPPORT PURCHASE	REENGAGE AND EMPOWER
Monitor buzz and shared passion	Build relationships with elite icitizens	Elevate engaged icitizens	Facilitate everyday icitizen interaction	Invite purchasers' CSI
Identify influence within and outside the brand	Deploy compelling interactive campaigns	Contribute to dialogue to ensure high SERPs	Accommodate multiple purchase modes	Provide stratified social rewards
		Provide CSI tools		

The role of the brand is to support and facilitate the consumers' multifaceted, circuitous journey.

Consumer as Medium and Message Also Means Cost Savings

Consumer behaviors in the belly of the fish are important for another reason. When consumers create, share and influence, in many instances, they become both a brand's message and the conduit for that message—its media. So, for the first time in the history of calculating the ROI of marketing expenditures, influence behaviors and patterns of the volume achievable only on the social web begin to offset the overall cost of marketing. Consumers can represent cost savings, not just sales.

MarketingSherpa awarded Levi Strauss (Hong Kong) a viral award because its "create-your-own-video" campaign around the theme of "How bold are you?" to promote Levi's TYPE 1 jeans yielded 474,000 video viewings in sixty days on YouTube alone, and moved marketshare for the jeans in Hong Kong from 13 percent to 33 percent—all through a largely CGM campaign. Levi's consumer-generated videos were accompanied by seeded, unbranded viral videos and banners, a microsite, print ads and wireless ring tones. But all of these spends, when aggregated with the inexpensive consumer videos, yielded a bigger bang for Levi's bucks.

The consumer as medium saves on distribution costs. The consumer as content creator saves on production costs. Using consumer-created content in 15-second ads, for instance, shaves about 75 percent off the near-$200,000 average cost for such a commercial with professional video, and it can be made in a fraction of the time. Major brands such as Chevrolet and Doritos have become so comfortable with user-created ads that by the end of 2006, they held high-profile contests for brand fans to create their Super Bowl TV commercials (the winners of which were aired during the big game in January 2007).

09:

The Love Triangle

We now know that push marketing has some serious competition from the digital millennials' strata of friends and icitizens' spontaneous communities—in short, the distinctly gregarious nature of the new fish-shaped consumer journey. Brands first have to join their conversations—a deceptively simple endeavor. They then can demonstrate the relevance of those conversations to an even broader consumer audience.

> *"No one could have envisioned what's happening today with the social media revolution. The powers-that-be have had a firm grip for so long they can't help but do a lockstep dance of communal denial. There has been more change in the way we communicate in the last eight years than in the previous 100 years—no question."*
>
> —**ED RAZEK**, CHIEF MARKETING OFFICER, LIMITED BRANDS

Far too often, though, brands are on the periphery of the icitizenry's shared passions, interests and homegrown expertise. A mere fraction of the videos on YouTube are brand-related. Despite the sophistication of SEO and SEM, brands are too frequently unassociated with common search words or phrases that serve as handy and indisputable signs of our zeitgeist. A routine search for "cool jeans for mom" or just "cool jeans," in June 2007, for instance, returned a couple SERPs (search engine results pages) of personal blogs and community sites but not a single brand or retailer, even as a paid listing.

Sometimes consumers' issues and sentiments become a groundswell of outreach or activism that can be a golden opportunity for marketers. When the blogosphere mobilized in early 2007 around the tainted pet food that reportedly led to thousands of animal deaths, brands had an opportunity to get it right about an emotional subject—the well-being of pets. But news about which brands were safe and unsafe and the numbers of pets sickened or killed trickled out from the source, Menu Foods (the manufacturer relied on by many brands), and the U.S. Food and Drug Administration. It was a missed opportunity for brands to offer, at minimum, some general nutritional advice and access to seasoned experts.

Have you ever thought about letting consumers develop your brand? What if magazines, TV shows and web sites allowed consumers to choose the brand sponsors and advertisers that matter most to them? How often would your brand be chosen? The internet provides a way to test how end users feel about a brand, a product and its messages. Experimenting with users on the web will help make any brand better. Test your products and messages and see the response. It is very hard for ten people in a conference room to guess what single message might connect with millions of consumers. It is really easy to rapidly test ten messages and get feedback from ten million people. Or better yet, ask ten million people what your brand message should be. Ask for help and you'll get it. What a beautiful thing.

—**TIM ARMSTRONG**, PRESIDENT,
ADVERTISING AND COMMERCE, GOOGLE

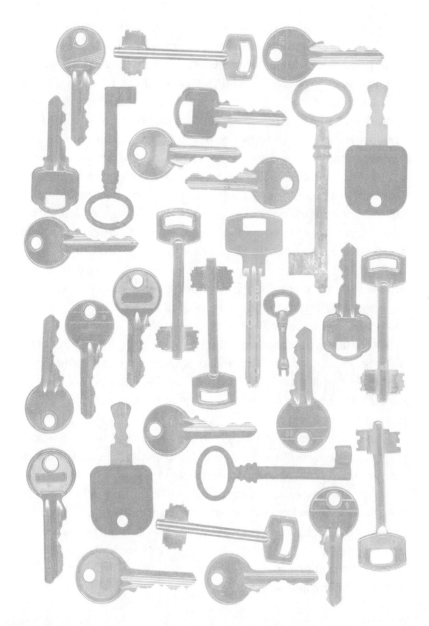

Instead, most brands let the category's relative newcomers or "amateurs" at Petconnection.com, Itchmo.com, Petsit.com and ThePetFoodList.com, among others, do all the organizing and talking—and organize they did. Petconnection.com even offered live blogging of the food-safety hearing in the U.S. House of Representatives. Where were the nation's trusted brands—Purina, Iams, Friskies—when panicked pet owners were clamoring for news?

The lesson here: keep your ear to the ground, know what your consumers care about and proactively provide relevant content. Marketers have a range of tools and third-party service providers of buzz monitoring and influence analysis at their disposal to learn what's being talked about the most, who's doing the talking and where. Such tools offer insights into everything from brand-relevant talk dispersion and volume to individual connectors and advocates. When combined with traditional consumer research, personas and segmentation schemes, brands can make their communications significantly more relevant, topical and timely.

Ultimately, open brand communications have to cast the brand as a member of a three-way relationship where push comes together with pull tactics, and all three parties—the brand, the consumer, online communities—meet at the shared intersection of passions and products.

The days of marketing locally to offline communities could have in no way prepared brands for the complexity and scale of the digital community dialogues they must join and enrich today.

Most consumer brands are still practicing B2C marketing. Now, they have to learn how to connect through a new relationship channel: B2We. By communicating with the vast and varied online communities (the "We") whose interests dovetail with those of the brand, companies can tap the connective tissue that now binds millions of consumers together.

Victoria's Secret Fashion Webcast Streams Love and Lingerie to the World

A soft launch of quite possibly the world's most awaited online shopping experience in late 1998 led to online orders from 37 countries in the first six hours of the ecommerce site's operation. But VictoriasSecret.com had still more up its peignoir sleeve.

In 1999, a Super Bowl commercial for the upcoming Victoria's Secret lingerie fashion show webcast drove one million sports fans (a third of Super Bowl fans are women) away from the halftime show and onto the web to learn more. Just 72 hours later, the world's first fashion show webcast took the internet by storm. Though confined rather unglamorously to a two inch video player, and plagued by multicasting issues at a time when streaming technologies were

not that sophisticated, the catwalk models still riveted. In just 21 minutes, lingerie—typically a private affair—found a rapt public eager to serve as audience. About 1.5 million viewers worldwide experienced the passion of lingerie as fashion and helped solidify the mutually sustaining triad—of personal sexiness and female confidence, worldwide fans of the brand and its (not to be overlooked) supermodels, and Victoria's Secret—that is the lifeblood of an open brand.

A bona fide pop culture phenomenon, *Brandweek* named the webcast and multimedia marketing blitz "Best Marketing Event of the Year."

RI CLIENT, 1998–PRESENT

There are no diminishing returns when brands think three-way, when they "triangulate" to communicate in a B2We world. Online communities are an infinite resource—ranging dramatically in size, duration, intimacy and credibility. They bring not only preexisting participants within the brand's range, but new icitizens formerly unaffiliated or uninvolved until their interest and passion is sparked by a marketing campaign or message that inspires them to join the brand ranks and spread the love. Consider how many new *Star Wars* fans will be drawn to the relaunched StarWars.com, thanks to Lucasfilm's decision to share more than 250 mashable clips from all six movies in the series, and even some state-of-the-art online video editing tools.

Triangulated communications don't just improve customer acquisition. They help marketers finally distinguish the different layers of consumers, from those who merely like the brand to those who adore it—the highest value icitizens. They also improve messaging effectiveness. Open brands can glean from online conversations—forums, message boards, blogs, reviews, social networking profiles, etc.—just what the world is thinking, dreaming and talking about. Not that the best brand marketers don't already have intuitive gifts for divining these currents; they now just have the evidence to back it up, thanks to the chatty, sharing nature of the social web.

So, three parties, three vertices in a triangle; this is what constitutes the ultimate open brand relationship. Not the Bermuda Triangle, mind you, into which brands seem to have disappeared instead of engaging in relevant cultural conversations, but a Love Triangle where individual consumers, the interlaced groupings of the icitizenry, and the brand come together strategically and organically through shared passions, ideas and interests.

OLD RELATIONSHIP MODEL

COMMUNITY

**ONLINE
OPPORTUNITY**

Brands once ruled the top of the triangle, pushing their messages
down to targeted consumers (and only occasionally to their communities).
Today's consumers and their communities (comprising the other two
vertices of the triangle) are often more engaged with each other than
with the brand directly on topics of interest.

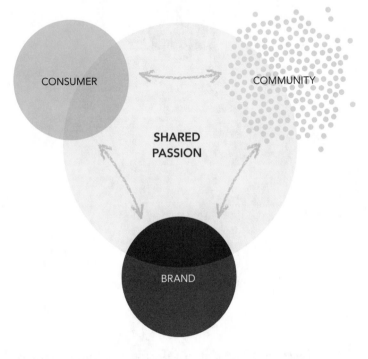

NEW RELATIONSHIP MODEL

CONSUMER

COMMUNITY

**SHARED
PASSION**

BRAND

To start feeling the love again, brands need to flip their
orientation from top to bottom so as to enable and engage in a
three-way dialogue that harnesses shared passion.

Playaway Pursues the Passion of Librarians

"We always knew that Playaway would have a certain appeal in the library channel. That said, what we failed to fully appreciate at the outset was the power of librarians themselves as a community of evangelists for our product. Some of an organization's best ideas come from the outside."
–Christopher Celeste, Founder and President, Findaway World, LLC

Findaway World, a company that produces Playaway portable audio books with built-in players, discovered the power of community when librarians checked out their product and couldn't stop whispering about it.

When Playaway went to their first library trade show, they realized that despite the channel's overall size (20,000+ public libraries and schools), this was an intimate, tightly connected group with a few key players who had megaphone-like volume within the community. By building relationships first with these individuals, without trying to control the flow, the startup was able to raise its visibility at an incredibly rapid pace.

Playaway launched a Library Advisory Group consisting of a cross-section of community members, which is designed not only to aid outbound brand messaging but, even more importantly, to impact the product evolution itself, from content selection to pricing to distribution to future product and packaging design. This initiative in particular is fueled by the recognition that librarians are not just sales prospects but literally partners in helping to build a better business model.

RI CLIENT, 2005–2006

PART III

Inside the Open Brand

10:

The Open Brand Framework

Are you ready to open?

If so, we've put together a strategic framework that capitalizes on both the social web's traits and technologies and the icitizenry's power to be both medium and message.

Two trends in particular anchor the open brand framework:

- The first is the emergence of consumer **notoriety** through the increased visibility of individuals—as data, as consumer profiles, as artists or entrepreneurs no longer reliant upon paid third parties to be "known" to the world. This is in contrast to what historically has been relative consumer **anonymity** with regard to brands and the world.
- The second is the emergence of **creative production**, the opposite of simple, uncritical **consumption**. This is evidenced by the dazzling array of engaging online activities that few twentieth century consumers enjoyed.

These two trends are on their way to becoming macrotrends whose impact will be felt beyond the digital universe. When we cast them as x- and y-axes on a grid, they frame four types of essential and interconnected consumer experiences—on-demand, personal, engaging and networked. Optimizing these consumer experiences in alignment with a brand's business objectives constitutes the way to open up to a web-made world.

Mapping this quartet of consumer experiences across the landscape of the social web also helps brands move away from

> "My research reveals that consumerism and the rampant consumption that goes with it has nearly run its course. People want a balance between consumption and creativity. Fortunately, the new communication and community-building technologies are helping to erode the old power structures and are giving a voice to people."
>
> —**LIZ SANDERS, Ph.D.**, FOUNDER, MAKETOOLS, LLC

the single, all-things-to-all-consumers "consumer experience" that makes brands seem closed and boxed in by their own rigid, often analog standards.

The ON-DEMAND EXPERIENCE is inspired by the digital competence-seeking icitizen—that time-starved consumer who views the internet as a life management tool and prefers relative anonymity as she seeks speed to information and task completion. This experience is characterized by efficiency, ease, control, findability and instantaneousness.

The PERSONAL EXPERIENCE takes its inspiration from the more celebrity-minded icitizen, who would expect a brand to foster a relationship with her. Within this experience, the brand enables individualized interaction, caters to her preferences and boosts her ability to influence others—and be recognized for doing so. This experience is characterized by acknowledgement, dialogue, customization, privilege and popularity.

The ENGAGING EXPERIENCE takes its cues from the collectively-motivated icitizens who want to be diverted and engrossed, and who develop an emotional attachment to brands that provide the means and occasions to shore up their social identities. An engaging experience satisfies consumers' desires to do more than acquire or observe. This experience is characterized by participation, belonging, immersion, entertainment and inspiration.

The NETWORKED EXPERIENCE is inspired by icitizens driven to effect cultural change, and who would expect a brand to do the same, primarily by engaging the social web's nodes of sharing and its seemingly limitless, unencumbered and portable paths to opportunity and innovation. The networked experience is valuable to those seeking creative and influential interactions, and would appeal to both the individual icitizen and icitizen communities. It also recognizes those icitizens' sense of entitlement about co-creating the brand's messages and offerings. The earmarks of the networked experience are self-expression, ego gratification, portability, community and meaningful change.

While the networked and personal experiences are shaped by the motivations of the elite icitizens, who are in fact a small portion of the icitizenry, the influence of these individuals is relatively greater because they're the new tastemakers—opinionated, passionate and iconoclastic. They shape improved experiences for everyday icitizens and even the rest of the online population because they're the de facto standard-bearers for open branding.

PRODUCTION
(of content and offerings)

ANONYMITY
(relative to brands and the world)

NOTORIETY
(relative to brands and the world)

CONSUMPTION
(of content and offerings)

ANONYMITY
(relative to brands and the world)

NOTORIETY
(relative to brands and the world)

ENGAGING
EXPERIENCE

Collectively-inclined
icitizens believe
"I CONNECT"

NETWORKED
EXPERIENCE

Cultural change
agents believe
"I AM"

ON-DEMAND
EXPERIENCE

Digital competence-
seeking icitizens believe
"I CAN"

PERSONAL
EXPERIENCE

Celebrity-motivated
icitizens believe
"I MATTER"

CONSUMPTION
(of content and offerings)

11

On-De

Efficiency.
Ease.
Control.
Findability.
Instantaneousness.

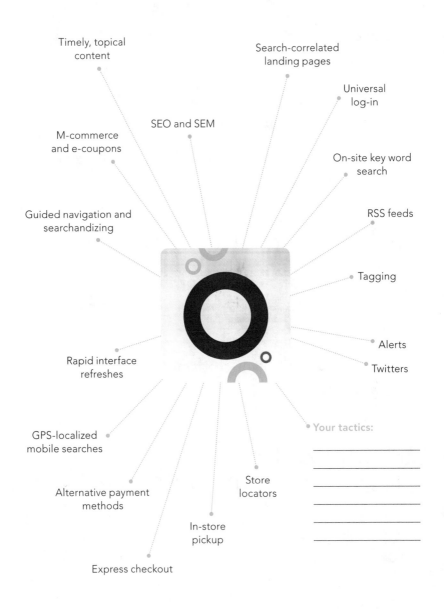

Timely, topical
content

Search-correlated
landing pages

Universal
log-in

SEO and SEM

M-commerce
and e-coupons

On-site key word
search

Guided navigation and
searchandizing

RSS feeds

Tagging

Rapid interface
refreshes

Alerts

Twitters

Your tactics:

GPS-localized
mobile searches

_____
_____
_____
_____
_____
_____

Alternative payment
methods

Store
locators

In-store
pickup

Express checkout

If your consumers can't find you (which means they're not buying from you)...

If speed to information or possession is a deciding factor in purchase...

If your consumers move back and forth frequently between channels pre- and post-purchase...

If your consumers want a range of payment methods...

If your conversion rates are low because you lack multiple product paths or consumer-centric filtering options...

If your consumers are increasingly reliant on mobile devices...

...PRIORITIZE THE ON-DEMAND EXPERIENCE!

For optimal brand openness, do this in conjunction with some fine-tuning of the other three consumer experiences, in the order of importance to your business objectives and growth opportunities.

The internet practically invented on-demand. Catalogs and call centers played a major role in whetting consumers' appetites for instant commerce. But it wasn't until e-commerce combined the visual clarity of catalogs with the real-time and personal information of a call center, and then added hyper-convenient search, payment and channel-synchronized functionality, that the on-demand concept took center stage, elevating brands that delivered well on this experience above those that did not.

An on-demand experience is about your brand being accessible to granular, long tail queries. According to an eTailing Group 2007 poll, about 71 percent of shoppers use keyword searches to find products, and many of those searches don't even include a brand name. Moreover, as many consumers arrive at your site via deep-linking from blogs, personal web pages and other media beyond your control, every page on your site should function as both your home page and a transaction page.

After you've made your site easy to find and hospitable on every page, your stores and products—including model, brand, color, size, style, format, availability and price—have to be eminently easy to find too. From any device, at any time. Orchestrating an on-demand experience also means reducing clicks; providing speedy screen loads and fast, reliable results; and easing the checkout process by storing customer information for one-click purchases and easy account status checks.

On-demand optimized brands must accommodate the multichannel consumer as well. When consumers "arrive" online, they expect an experience that relates to the message or cue that drove them there, whether a URL on packaging, a broadcast campaign, radio ads that invite opt-ins, email blasts, bag stuffers or other promotions. Mobile consumers will expect more personal utility from their devices, including mobile interfaces for brand web sites, coupon receipt and redemption, and transactions.

The following are a few standout brands providing fast, frictionless on-demand experiences:

GAP'S QuickLook is a mini-product window that lets shoppers see inventory availability, select size and color, and add to the cart while still on the same page. Shoppers remain in control of their environment and can easily browse alternatives without delays due to page loads or navigation confusion.

SEARS' in-store pickup service allows consumers to purchase online and then get their items at their local Sears, forgoing checkout lines and shipping costs. A post-purchase email confirms product availability so that impatient shoppers can head to the mall for (almost) immediate gratification.

Paul Miller, Senior Vice President, Direct Commerce, Sears Holdings Corp, notes: "The 'Ready in 5 Guaranteed' program ensures an online order will be ready in five minutes for in-store pickup or customers receive a $5 gift card. If the item isn't ready in 10 minutes, a $10 gift card, and so on. This builds trust and loyalty, particularly with our time-pressed customers who expect a frictionless experience."

GOOGLE Checkout streamlines purchase by enabling consumers to use one name and password for all retail partner sites. Once consumers enter their billing information, they can practically check out with one click. They can also track all their orders in one place. Google Checkout also lets users choose whether to keep their email addresses confidential, and lets them opt out of unwanted email from merchants.

FANDANGO makes it easy for consumers to find a movie using their mobile devices. After going to mobile.fandago.com, consumers just type in a zip code and select a theater. Their mobile device then displays movies and show times for the theater. Moviegoers can also check out alerts, movie reviews and maps, to have all the information they need for a night on the town.

GATHER is a social media site that attracts novice and professional artists and writers alike by compensating those that publish everything from articles to photos. The site revolves around tags that each contributor uses to identify the subject matter of her entry. Also described as "the living index of all content on Gather," tags make it easy for users to sort through massive amounts of information to find relevant content.

ZILLOW provides ease and efficiency to real estate market consumers with state-of-the-art online tools for buying and selling homes. Features like online property searches, property listing, and Zestimate (estimated market value) make it easy for buyers and sellers to find the information they need quickly. The Make Me Move feature allows users to post the price for which they'd like to sell their home, opening the door for buyers to find their (affordable) dream home. The site's navigability and findability gives consumers the power to research, buy and sell real estate without relying on newspapers or agents.

For more, or to contribute your own, visit www.theopenbrand.com.

Walmart.com is Catalyst for More Consumer Ease, Control and Choice

When Wal-Mart undertook one of the most encompassing web site redesigns in the online retail industry, it had its 130 million customers in mind, particularly the 75% who are already active online. Improved information hierarchies, more intuitive navigation, cleaner and bolder design, enhanced search and natural search engine optimization, and better labeling and photography made for greater ease in the digital shopping experience. Fewer clicks and faster transactions have led to higher average order sizes and more happy, smiling digital customers. Following the site's redesign, Walmart.com scaled the Nielsen/Net Ratings ranks of the ten largest online shopping sites, moving from No. 7 to No. 3—registering 23 million unique visitors in January 2007 alone, up 25 percent from the previous year. Walmart.com has also shown significant improvements in brand perception; ratings across all brand attributes have increased, with "innovative," "trustworthy" and "knowledgeable" showing the largest upsurge.

In addition to the site redesign, Wal-Mart rolled out nationally a Site to Store service at Walmart. com that offers free shipping on more products than are available in-store to customers. The retailer learned from consumer research that store customers, despite the fact that they shop an average of 70 times a year, often only have time to shop for what they need and not for what they want in such product categories as home and baby. Store customers also wanted more products from which to choose in categories such as consumer electronics. Early indications are that the new Site to Store service thoroughly addresses these time-strapped yet variety-conscious consumers' needs. Only a few months after the national rollout, this on-demand feature is responsible for a third of the retailer's online sales, and 60 percent of customers who order on Walmart.com and pick up items in the local store purchase an additional $60 worth of goods at the store.

RI CLIENT, 2005–PRESENT

12

Person

Acknowledgement.

Dialogue.

Customization.

Privilege.

Popularity.

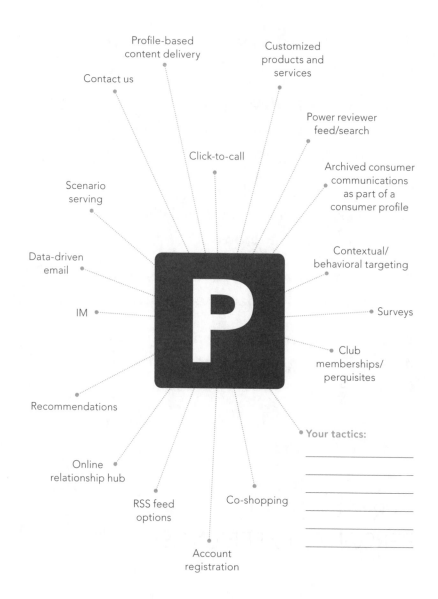

Profile-based content delivery

Customized products and services

Contact us

Power reviewer feed/search

Click-to-call

Archived consumer communications as part of a consumer profile

Scenario serving

Data-driven email

Contextual/ behavioral targeting

IM

Surveys

P

Club memberships/ perquisites

Recommendations

Your tactics:

Online relationship hub

RSS feed options

Co-shopping

Account registration

If your consumers expect human interaction for guidance and support...

If you haven't yet leveraged your content and customer data to deliver a more targeted consumer experience...

If you need to expand the ways your consumer can experience your brand socially, as part of the privileged in-crowd...

If you haven't provided tools for consumers to routinely share feedback, ratings and reviews...

If your consumers aren't shopping multiple categories or are at a spending threshold (perhaps they are not rewarded for loyalty)...

If your consumers' registered profile information isn't being shared across channels...

...PRIORITIZE THE PERSONAL EXPERIENCE!

In the personal experience, brands begin a genuine conversation with individuals who are much closer to notoriety on the social web's anonymity-to-notoriety continuum. They want to be known and valued by the brand network, so there should be ongoing interaction between people, not just computers or loyalty cards. Consumers craving a personal experience expect more customized products and services, synchronization of their browsing and purchasing behavior, and acknowledgment of their patronage.

In many organizations, such efforts to know and respond to individual consumers might already be enabled by a CRM program with updated and integrated databases. Yet treating customers as individuals requires more than a technology strategy. For most brands, it requires a new kind of business strategy born of a fundamental shift in thinking.

Within the personal experience, brands convert active listening into solutions, recommendations, reminders, invitations, thank-you's and—when things don't go smoothly—apologies. Communications should abandon canned corporate-speak in favor of messages that are—or at least feel—personal, reflective and spontaneous. Companies seeking to deepen customer relationships must not only invest in the infrastructure that integrates unconnected customer databases, but also spend more time staying with consumers by thoughtfully engaging them even after providing requested information or a resolution to a problem.

Preparing for more personalized dialogues means moving beyond the superficial gesture of requesting consumer feedback. A brand optimized for the personal experience acknowledges consumer opinions and concerns, then processes the feedback, integrates it with the consumer's brand history, shares it with departments beyond sales and, finally, institutes genuine changes where appropriate because of it. Imagine streaming, real-time customer feedback scrolling across the computer screens of every associate in your business.

The personal experience also uses the digital channel to heighten analog privileges—special services, communications and events that transcend the basic business of shopping and purchasing—and enhance the popularity of consumers who value it.

The following are brands whose personal experience clearly puts the human relationship with consumers front and center:

MINI COOPER makes the car-buying experience personal, fun and interactive. Since more than 70 percent of MINIs are customized, soon-to-be owners must wait for their MINI to be manufactured and shipped. But instead of the typical 6- to 8-week lull between the down payment and the delivery, MINI keeps its buyers engaged with a personalized online tracking service that manages buyer expectations while creating anticipation for the celebrated arrival.

LANDS' END LIVE was one of the first customer knowledge services offered by a major online retailer in 1996. Designed to bridge the gap between a shopper with a question and a brand representative with an answer, it enabled consumers to choose how they wanted to engage in a customer support dialogue—by phone, email or live online chat. This near-instant exchange serves as a trust-builder by providing timely reassurance, clarification and support.

KASHI invites dialogue with health-conscious online fans by sharing its employees' inspiring stories of personal transformation, which are filled with wellness goals, barriers and motivations.

HP Gets Personal

Hewlett-Packard (HP) has been leading the charge of B2B marketing with its "Technology At Work" e-newsletter. The initiative, which launched in 2001, now influences over $100 million in customer spending while simultaneously saving HP millions of dollars by enabling self-help for customers. HP's newsletter goes beyond selling, providing value-added tips for using products that customers already own, along with news, event announcements and promotions based on customer profiles.

This proactive email alert has helped HP strengthen post-purchase customer loyalty. Explains Paul Horstmeier, Vice President, HP.com Marketing Services, "We applied a rating system of 1–5 to most of our articles, then tracked the content quality ratings each month. We also published and communicated the results of the content articles each month back to the content providers, as well as consulted with them, to help improve the overall content quality. Ultimately the success of an e-newsletter program depends on the quality of the content, and the personalization engine and capabilities to deliver good content to the right person."

RI CLIENT, 1997–Present

In turn, site visitors are encouraged to make and share a transformation in their own lives, which others can view, tag and search by geography and recency. Once the dialogue has been initiated with a simple sign-up page, Kashi poses three simple survey questions to determine its influencers. They offer coupons to those who engage on the site and share more personal information, and invite some users to join testing panels. Kashi also extends its warm, welcoming tone in the "Contact Us" section of its site by featuring customer service representatives' photos and using inviting explanatory copy.

After SHAW INDUSTRIES introduced a state-of-the-art visualization feature, Try On A Floor, to their site www.shawfloors. com, they deepened the personal experience with an "Upload Your Own Room" enhancement. The free, web-based photo upload feature allows consumers to easily customize pics of their own rooms by trying different flooring options, including carpet, laminate, hardwood, ceramic and area rugs, and even allows consumers to change the colors of their walls, cabinets and other surfaces. Once a room is designed, consumers can send their "My Shaw Floors" selections to friends and family for review and commentary. An ad campaign to launch the manufacturer's new site feature enabled consumers to actually begin building their own room in-banner before they ever reached the Shaw site.

For more, or to contribute your own, visit www.theopenbrand.com.

13

Engag

Participation.
Belonging.
Immersion.
Entertainment.
Inspiration.

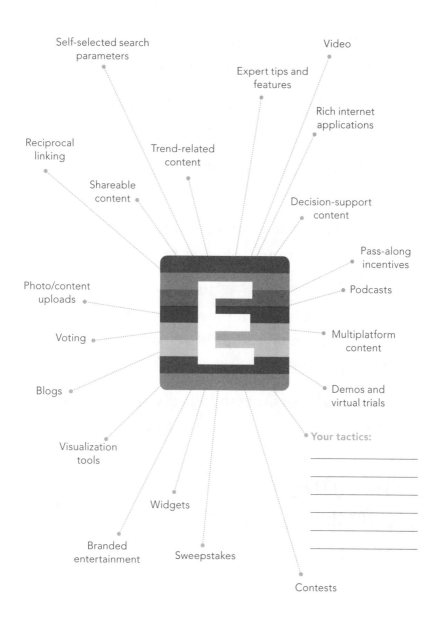

Self-selected search parameters

Video

Expert tips and features

Rich internet applications

Reciprocal linking

Trend-related content

Shareable content

Decision-support content

Pass-along incentives

Photo/content uploads

Podcasts

Voting

Multiplatform content

Blogs

Demos and virtual trials

Visualization tools

Your tactics:

Widgets

Branded entertainment

Sweepstakes

Contests

If your digital marketing doesn't provide emotionally involving content and interactivity...

If your brand needs to come to life via video and rich internet applications...

If your target market is inspired by gaming and other interactive adventures...

If your products and services could be more "knowable" and more relevant to individual lifestyles...

If your content is less timely, topical and available than your competitors' and elite icitizens' content ...

If your brand message and media are not worthy of sharing or passing along...

...PRIORITIZE THE ENGAGING EXPERIENCE!

While an optimized on-demand experience helps consumers accomplish objectives more quickly and effortlessly, the engaging experience focuses on the opposite: elongating the brand experience. It aims to increase dwell time by making each site visit, mobile feed and online campaign fresh, enriching and entertaining (when appropriate). Engaging experiences should be so deeply involving that the consumer gets happily "lost" in interaction and discovery, and wants to share her experience with others.

The engaging experience uses triggers and tactics from the conventional arsenal of emotional brand-building—luscious, vivid photography; video and sound; and clever copy with compelling narrative hooks. But engaging experiences also require calls to action, inspirational starting points, enticing pathways for exploration and discovery, and other sticky attributes that yield less formulaic, more relevant consumer explorations.

Fully engaging a consumer also means enhancing her ability to see and experience a product within the context of her world (such as a convincing equivalent of her body or home). While the consumer's objective is to minimize purchase risk—online and offline—it's an engaging brand's job to maximize consumer confidence by creating pathways for educational, empowering and emotional connections.

The following brands boast engaging experiences that are immersive enough to encourage a consumer's further exploration and deepening emotional bond with it and with other brand fans:

CNN'S "News to Me" is the first cable news show devoted purely to user-generated content (UGC). Debuting in May 2007, the weekly show is a compendium of the best online videos, news coverage and other content created by icitizens (and/or submitted by CNN viewers). CNN has become a major media leader in

Herbal Essences Dumps Cupid

In a fun-loving campaign that resulted in one of Procter & Gamble's most popular brand web sites, Herbal Essences took aim at the romantic myths of Valentine's Day's iconic cherub. The campaign and site were based on a key consumer insight that many women who are dateless on that day dread the holiday. The site introduced a comically inept Cupid to spark conversations within Herbal Essences' target market about love gone astray—and the power of beautiful hair to smooth romance's crooked path.

This multichannel, fully integrated campaign was seeded on YouTube two weeks prior to launch without additional media promotion; two of the three videos had garnered more than a million views within seven weeks. Viewers were driven to an interactive microsite where they enjoyed mockumentary footage of Cupid in action, shared their best and worst Valentine's Day stories, played games and sent e-valentines.

The Dump Cupid campaign was supported by a 30-foot arrow in Times Square, TV and out-of-home advertising, radio endorsements and an online sweepstakes. The campaign also used rich media ads (via a Yahoo home page takeover on Valentine's Day, plus sponsorships with MySpace and YouTube) that reached more than 90 million visitors globally in a single week.

RI CLIENT, 2006-PRESENT

tapping the power of the icitizenry to engage in major issues of the day, staging the revolutionary "CNN/YouTube Debates," which featured videotaped questions posed to 2008 presidential candidates by YouTube users.

Although a digital-only wonder, and with very little paid media, PHILLIPS NORELCO Bodygroom razor campaign cut through the clutter of the usual marketing blather about blades with its ShaveEverywhere.com site. Its viral success made the Bodygroom the company's second-best-selling product, representing 25 percent of dollar sales and tripled projections. The site features a live-action spokesman delivering a humorous monologue about the more private places where men shave—and the even more private reasons why. Over 2.8 million visitors have explored the site since its May 2006 debut.

WEBMD might never replace a visit to the doctor but it does provide in-depth health information, and features over 90 lifestyle and conditions areas, online communities with expert-led message boards, peer-to-peer forums and live events. With more than 40 million unique visitors a month, WebMD provides a place for people to ask questions and find answers about health and wellness, and connect with others who are dealing with the same issues. By providing decision-supportive content, an appreciative and engaged audience has made it the fastest-growing and most-visited health site on the internet.

STEPHEN KING fans looking forward to his horror novel, *Cell*, were highly engaged by a mobile marketing campaign that allowed users to join the Stephen King VIP Club, receive a voice message from Stephen King himself, as well as weekly text messages chock-full of wallpaper with jackets of the book, trivia, sweepstakes and polls. But because *Cell* involves an *Invasion of the Body Snatchers*-type plot, two talk-tones were for sale that brought the listener into the intrigue; in one, the author ominously intones, "The next call you take may be your last." The campaign marks the first time a major book publisher used a mobile marketing campaign for an adult title and the first time that a book publisher included a revenue-generating component in a book launch.

Despite his pseudo-right wing broadcast personality's trademark obliviousness, STEPHEN COLBERT knows better than almost any TV star how to use the web for brand-building. Since naming Wikipedia his favorite web site on *The Colbert Report* on July 31, 2006, Colbert has coined several words with 'wiki' in them, hosted Wikipedia founder Jimmy Wales on his show, and invited his fans to follow his example and change certain entries—including "elephants" and "George Washington" and the one for Colbert himself—to suit their version of reality (wikiality). His web site, www.colbertnation.com, generates fan content that he occasionally features on his show, including homemade *Star Wars* videos with Colbert himself as hero, made in response to his show's "Green-screen Challenge." He also rallied online voters in August 2006 to name a Hungarian bridge after himself—and almost succeeded.

For more, or to contribute your own, visit www.theopenbrand.com.

"Price, durability, stain resistance, color. This is how the industry traditionally talked to our consumer about flooring. It's viewed as a commodity and how many people get emotional about commodities? The key now is inspiring her to view the floor as something more, and helping her see that the quickest way to change the look/feel/emotion of a room is by changing the flooring. We use the web to educate her about flooring and equip her with the latest tools to visualize her dream home."

—**SCOTT SANDLIN**, VP HARD SURFACE BUSINESS DEVELOPMENT (FORMERLY VP MARKETING), SHAW INDUSTRIES

14

Netwo

Self-expression.
Ego gratification.
Portability.
Community.
Meaningful change.

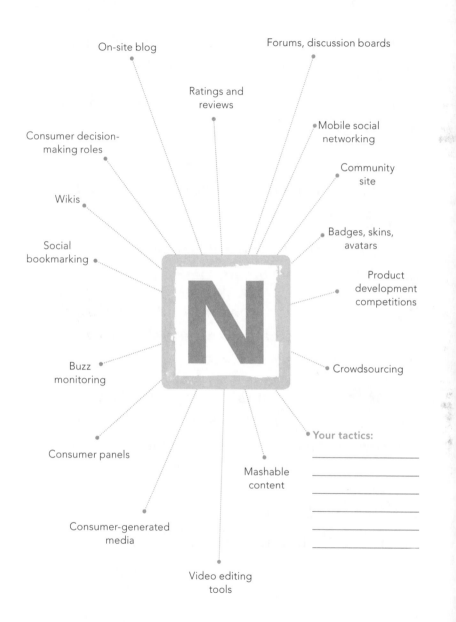

On-site blog

Forums, discussion boards

Ratings and reviews

Mobile social networking

Consumer decision-making roles

Community site

Wikis

Badges, skins, avatars

Social bookmarking

Product development competitions

Buzz monitoring

Crowdsourcing

Your tactics:

Consumer panels

Mashable content

_____

_____

_____

Consumer-generated media

_____

_____

_____

Video editing tools

If your consumers want to share their opinions and ideas, and be recognized for doing so...

If your consumers want to react to and interact with other consumers' contributions...

If you aren't mining and monitoring the digital landscape for the next icitizens to represent or personify your brand...

If your brand isn't keeping pace with the most digitally savvy consumers' desire for DIY tools...

If your category is stagnating and feels closed to consumer co-creation and the abundance of goodwill on the social web...

If your consumer wants the opportunity to co-appear with your brand or its products wherever she has a presence online...

...PRIORITIZE THE NETWORKED EXPERIENCE!

The fourth in this set is the networked experience, which embraces consumers and communities of consumers as a profound part of brand building, inviting them to co-create and co-appear with the brand at the relevant nodes of the social web. In the process, elite icitizens for the brand emerge as key assets because, through the "strength of weak ties," they can raise broad awareness of the brand, product or service.

The networked experience might sound familiar to brands that have invited select consumers into their inner sanctum through focus groups and brand advisory panels. These conventional, controlled approaches to co-creation take on a new scale and immediacy when the internet is leveraged as a platform for recruiting, interacting and assimilating consumer-generated ideas and input.

Either through official brand sites, or "unofficial" platforms for participation, brand fans can be targeted and enticed to get creative about influencing everything from the look and feel of a brand to its future offerings. Whether seeking input on a campaign, product development, or solutions to specific problems within the existing business, brands willing to open up to consumer participation will find a vast pool of volunteers ready to offer assistance and inspiration.

The networked experience is essentially about fostering relationships with elite icitizens and their communities to achieve meaningful results for the brand. These relationships begin with the tools or resources for consumer/brand co-creation, and are sustained by the brand's public embrace of these consumer contributions. Many elite icitizens who are eager to amplify their opinions and experiences can be motivated through competitions with monetary awards. Most, however, desire simple (but public) acknowledgement that they represent or embody the brand.

The following brands provide networked experiences that enable brand co-creation:

NETFLIX publicly acknowledged its desire to improve the DVD renters' recommendations engine—a key driver of higher movie selection that has been instrumental in driving customer loyalty and participation. Instead of hiring pricey consultants or relying solely on their in-house developers, they offered a $1 million prize to the team that could best improve the recommendations' relevancy by at least 10 percent. This invitation creates a competitive opportunity for some of the best programmers across the world to show what they can do, while also limiting the potential risk for many costly trials and errors in development.

PETCO realized that ratings and reviews could help trigger consumer interaction and peer support. To build its inventory of reviews quickly, PETCO incentivized its customers with a "chance to win" promotion that garnered an 800 percent increase in participation. Once the ratings and reviews reached critical mass, the company was quickly able to identify low-rated products; it also allowed customer service representatives to proactively reach out to dissatisfied customers. In addition, PETCO was able to identify top-rated products and, by marketing those products as customer favorites, increase consumer buying confidence, conversion rates and average order sizes.

AMERICAN EXPRESS Cardmember benefits have expanded beyond typical perks and privileges. The American Express Members' Project invited the member community to shape the brand by sharing innovative, achievable ideas with the potential to make a positive impact on the world. Their motto, "Our money.

> *"There will be convergence and availability of user-generated content, such as ratings and reviews, through several devices, such as the mobile phone, in-store kiosks and POS systems (or other devices a salesperson can carry). In-store signage will likely feature ratings more than reviews. It is just a matter of time when the web will be so ubiquitous that accessing this kind of content in any channel will be the norm."*
>
> —BRETT HURT, CEO, BAZAARVOICE

Your ideas. Your decision." was supported by the company's pledge of up to $5 million to bring the best idea to life. The three-month project allowed cardmembers to submit ideas as well as to explore, rate and discuss the collective submissions, and then vote for the winning idea.

THREADLESS is the rare retailer that relies almost exclusively on its community for product development and marketing. The community submits designs and decides which tee shirts should be produced for sale. Not only has Threadless effectively grown its brand in an otherwise commoditized product category, it has created a dynamic shopping experience that changes daily based on the contributions of its fans. It draws repeat traffic from those submitting designs, buying tee shirts and casting votes, as well as from those simply seeking to stay abreast of the latest trends. Sales are an instant litmus test of marketplace taste.

PONTIAC teamed with Yahoo! to launch Pontiac Underground, an online destination for Pontiac owners and enthusiasts. A Yahoo! Autos study found that 94 percent of respondents who use the web said they believe consumer-generated content is an important source when making buying decisions, so Pontiac wanted to support and connect its existing but disparate communities via such content. Pontiac Underground centralizes Pontiac-related content from various Yahoo! products such as Flickr (photos), Yahoo! Answers and Yahoo! Video, and integrates links from outside Yahoo! in conjunction with its "Inside Track" blog and other social media tools. The site also offers RSS feeds of user posts from niche advocacy groups into the broader clubs area of the site.

STARWOOD's aloft Hotels previewed its new hotel concept in the Second Life virtual world. Avatars were invited to explore and comment on floor plans, decor, amenities, gathering places such as the lobby, bar and restaurant; and even to take a dip in the pool. And for the millions of future aloft Hotel customers that have not yet created an avatar or didn't visit this virtual universe, and to boost its PR efforts, aloft (wisely) used a blog to log its online construction process—complete with time-lapse photography, 3D modeling and visitor comments.

For more, or to contribute your own, visit www.theopenbrand.com.

Intuit's Networking Intuitions

Intuit's Online Community grew out of its members' desire to interact more substantially with each other, and to have a greater voice in product development. According to Scott K. Wilder, Group Manager, Intuit Online Communities, "We led the charge in community-building with our Web 2.0 community because we discovered that over fifty percent of our users were coming to our e-commerce web site for information."

Members have access to blogs, can search for local service providers and are invited to post product feedback (to which Intuit responds in a public forum). Since its inception, dozens of changes have been made to Intuit's Quickbooks software based on user feedback. In addition, heavy users are deemed "All Stars" and are routinely invited into a private forum where they preview products and provide input to the company.

Continues Wilder: "We designed a legal training program for the company called 'How to use an online community.' It consists of how-to's, legal aspects, privacy issues. Most companies put great effort to training senior executives, but they rarely extend the same training to the rest of the company."

Intuit offers an opt-in program, given once per quarter in multiple cities, and a 'Train the Trainer' program, which allows customization for business units.

"The biggest learning we've had is that it's a user community. We need to partner with them to find out what works well and what we could do better. "

15:

Opened Up

By now you must be thinking: just how open should my brand be? Slightly ajar for the bracing breezes of feedback-happy consumers? Wide open to all comers? If open is good, then wide open must be better, right?

Yes and no.

Open brands are strategically opened, emphasizing one or two consumer experiences that most represent value to be captured, and disruptive change that will keep competitors following fast. Brands have to find their "sweet spot" through a careful assessment of their four consumer experiences and the technological innovations that support them—how both stack up to their consumers' expectations and to the competition. Knowing where a brand stands currently and where it should go requires prioritizing experiences—and their corresponding open brand tactics—as OPEN (on-demand is most important because too many of my consumers bail during checkout). Or perhaps as NOPE (networked AND on-demand constitute the way forward because my target market is millennials and my competitor doesn't know the first thing about m-commerce), or maybe even PONE. No matter their order, the open brand's four essential consumer experiences should be enabled based on your priorities.

One brand that hits the mark with all four experiences, but truly excels at delivering engaging experiences (ENOP) is *American Idol*, a mega-hit spawned by the 2001 UK reality series, *Pop Idol*. With its democratic twist and skyrocketing success, *American Idol* and its parent company, 19 Entertainment, have used open branding to discover and create the world's next pop stars.

Idol's formula has attracted mixed-age audiences, bringing together families, friends and colleagues by delivering in each of the four open experiences (though with an emphasis on the engaging experience due to its TV-based "home"). Its audience is activated by voting, blogging, word of mouth, discussion boards and entertaining pass-along videos.

AMERICAN IDOL

ENGAGING

- Participants share relatable personal stories on each show (along with singing a song)
- Controversial judges create buzz-worthy tension that goads viewers
- Guest performances from superstars in many musical styles, from Prince and Jennifer Lopez to Tony Bennett and Bon Jovi, draw a diverse audience
- Online exit interviews with contestants, season recaps, backstage videos, ring tones, etc. keep the audience engaged when the TV is off

NETWORKED

- Viewers have the power of collective decision-making; they "create" the next star with their votes
- Contestants amplify the hype by writing entertaining blogs that provoke consumer interaction and discussion
- Fans are inspired to create their own sites, with forums, predictions, custom content and opinions that fuel the franchise

ON-DEMAND

- Accessible to watch (or TiVo) via FOX network in prime time
- Easy to cast a vote via toll-free number and text messaging
- Viewable anytime online

PERSONAL

- Casting process across the U.S. includes thousands of hopefuls from all walks of life
- Show "feels" personal as contestants return weekly based on viewer input, creating a vested interest among viewers
- Online membership includes blogs, avatars, favorites lists and other custom perks

Never a brand to sit idly on the sidelines, Nike has been augmenting its mega brand-building strategy of catapulting superstar athletes onto the stage of cultural icons. It's opening up online to amateur athletes, teams and their like-minded communities.

Nike's ever-evolving digital experience is testament to its avoidance of formulaic solutions. Consider how Nike+ shoes, in combination with Apple's iPod nano, serve as a virtual personal trainer. The shoes' sensor communicates via a receiver plugged into the nano and a voice (male or female) describes the runner's stats, calories burned, and distance remaining.

Opening all four consumer experiences, but particularly the personal one, makes Nike+ a runner's dream:

ENGAGING

- Compelling visual design and interactivity invite dwell time and discovery
- Nike-endorsed athletes are portrayed in video describing the song that motivates them to work out
- Workout mixes designed for different routines and durations can be downloaded to an iPod
- PowerSongs (favorite song for an extra boost) are voted for and featured online

NETWORKED

- Runners can challenge as many as 100 people to compete against each other or invite them to form a team
- Individual and shared goals can be organized and tracked
- Distance Club encourages runners to share a personal milestone and favorite PowerSong, linked to iTunes for easy purchase
- An online forum and blog provokes discussion and content sharing

ON-DEMAND

- Easy access to running routes filtered by distance and geography
- Rapid screen refreshes ensure satisfying interactive experience
- Goals Widget provides instantaneous progress updates
- Quick links to related apparel and accessories in the NikeStore

PERSONAL

- Runs are automatically tracked at nikeplus.com
- Runners can express their personal style by customizing made-to-order Nike+ shoes
- Enables custom iPod mixes for easy download

Webkinz from GANZ is another open brand firing on all experiential pistons. Not simply a line of collectible stuffed animals, Webkinz is a toy phenomenon triggered by the appeal of its personalized, interactive online playground. Each stuffed animal (enjoyed primarily by kids 5–11) comes with a secret code. When kids type in their unique code at Webkinz.com, they "adopt" a pet avatar that looks like the stuffed one they own.

Webkinz is not just a highly personal experience but a thoroughly engaging one as well. It has raised the bar for interactivity with the youth market while bridging the gap between the physical and virtual worlds:

INSIDE THE OPEN BRAND

WEBKINZ

ENGAGING

- Daily, one-time spins on the Wheel of Wow, weekly contests and other scheduled and surprise activities invite interaction and repeat visits
- Collectible trading cards encourage offline interaction and fun
- Archivable and printable wish list provides a handy shopping list for parents

NETWORKED

- Friends can be challenged in the tournament area
- Standardized messages and a restricted dictionary provide safe ways for kids to interact through their avatars
- Items accumulated using KinzCash can be shared with friends
- Catalyzes offline networking in after-school programs and neighborhood play groups by allowing limited online access and emphasizing engaging and personal experiences

ON-DEMAND

- Immediate access to a bank of KinzCash upon registry ensures interaction with the environment
- Points earned from games played are instantly tallied and accessible for virtual transactions
- Fast site access allows for satisfying interactions even if time is limited

PERSONAL

- Kids can play arcade games and perform a "job" to win more KinzCash to support and accessorize their pets
- Happiness, health and hunger meters show kids how well they are caring for their pets
- Kids earn KinzCash by answering simple survey questions

PINK, Victoria's Secret's breakaway lifestyle collection, has innovated across all four consumer experience types for its young female adult and older teen audience. Extending the store experience using event marketing—including its Rally at the Raleigh and the World's Largest PJ Party—the brand then extends from offline to online, viral and mobile; and to an increasingly qualified audience. The PJ Party delivered a 400 percent increase in qualified site traffic and five times the normal conversion rate, and exemplifies being highly engaging and optimally opened up:

VICTORIA'S SECRET PINK

RI CLIENT, 2006–PRESENT

ENGAGING

- The PJ Party featured vocalist Fergie, and special guests Kristin Cavallari and DJ AM
- Vspink.com included a Fergie bio page with streaming music, an interactive Chicago guide, party itinerary, DJ AM's iTunes playlist and a Contest Winner page
- Event venue was transformed to reflect the PINK brand with oversized stuffed dogs, pink blankets and bleachers, a photo booth and PINK pop-up shop

NETWORKED

- A dance video upload contest set to Fergie's latest hit yielded consumer participation beyond predictions
- PINK fans voted on who should win
- SMS announcements about free merchandise created flashmob experiences for PJ Party guests

ON-DEMAND

- PJ Party tickets were downloadable from vspink.com
- Site visitors can sign up for an RSS feed of PINK announcements, invitations, etc.
- AIM users can adopt PINK-branded icons

PERSONAL

- A mobile photo blog at the event enabled partygoers to send pictures from their mobile phones. Their candid photos (and selves) were projected onto the stage's LED screen and simultaneously posted on vspink.com
- Additional PJ Party invitations were delivered by PINK street teams to lucky individuals
- The video dance contest winner received a shopping spree from PINK and her video was featured on vspink.com
- Vspink.com offers content for personal web pages on MySpace and Facebook

PART IV

Getting to Open

16:

Opening
Measures

During this transitional period from closed to open, the web has become a bona fide brand-building channel in addition to a direct response vehicle. It has unleashed an extensive world of consumer engagement before an industry long focused simply on achieving consumer exposure to ads, all of which has prompted marketers to speak of relationship-building as the new imperative, not just "telling and selling," in the words of P&G's Global CMO Jim Stengel.

It has sprouted enough winding peer-to-peer or consumer-to-third-party paths to purchase to have rendered the traditional brand-controlled marketing funnel a relic. A marketing productivity measurement system right for this moment, then, would have to be equally transitional and contain these contradictions. It would have to be a judicious blend of foundational and emerging metrics.

Though it's not easy setting up a barometer of success when encamped at the frontlines of a revolution, the O.P.E.N. paradigm is built for change. Its four-part foundation both ensures prioritization and encourages experimentation. It helps attune a brand to an online population itself very much in transition. An O.P.E.N. metrics system accommodates a millennial cohort that experiences the web as a social phenomenon but also accommodates X'ers and boomers, 45 percent of whom are seeking mainly to be digitally proficient at their various tasks. All icitizens are part of the revolutionary changes underway, but as we've seen from our motivational research, their reasons for using the web could not be more different. And an open brand is, if anything, responsive to these icitizen reasons.

The O.P.E.N. system first ties the consumer experience deemed most important by a brand to a common business objective. Whatever consumer experience the brand is optimizing—on-demand, personal, engaging or networked—then provides its own metrics priorities. The following grid, though certainly not comprehensive, shows how the O.P.E.N. system is organized:

THE OPEN BRAND METRICS SYSTEM

CONSUMER EXPERIENCE	BUSINESS OBJECTIVE	FOUNDATIONAL METRICS	EMERGING METRICS
ON-DEMAND	Conversion/Sales	• CTR (Click-Through Rate) • Conversion Rate • Email Open Rate • Page Load Time • Bounce Rate • Abandonment Rate	• Task Completion Rate • Browse-to-Buy Ratio • View-Through • RSS Adoption
PERSONAL	Retention/Loyalty	• RFM (Recency, Frequency, Monetary) • CLV (Customer Lifetime Value) • Customer Satisfaction Score • Registered Accounts • Return Visits	• Profile Extension • Mobile Opt-In Rate • Advanced Attitudinal • Percent User-Generated Content • Visitor Investment Index • On-Site Influencer Score • Individual Social Media Index
ENGAGING	Awareness/Trial	• Site Visit Duration • Content Group Duration • Unique Visitors • Opt-In • Impressions	• Sentiment • Purchase Intent • Favoriting/Bookmarking • Content Consumption • Duration-Satisfaction
NETWORKED	Awareness/ Customer Acquisition	• Send to a Friend • Non-Search Engine-Referred Traffic • Share of Voice	• Attributed Conversions • Aggregated Postings Volume • Buzz Monitoring • Net Promoter Score • Pass-along Rate • Content Propagation

ON-DEMAND **foundational metrics, as we can see, are primarily consumer behavior metrics, and include the oldest and most basic, online and off.** They help measure marketing's ability to prompt a desired behavior—say, a newsletter signup or the viewing of a video in-banner, often called a "conversion" in the general sense—and, ultimately, to generate a sale.

- The classic Recency, Frequency and Monetary (RFM) metric is a way of measuring (and projecting) customer value based on documented interactions and purchases.

- The digital metric trinity for the last decade is still valuable: it's comprised of link-based Click-Through Rates (CTR), online Conversion Rates and Email Open Rates. Click-Through and Conversion Rates are usually part of the analytics package for a Pay Per Click (PPC) campaign.

- Page Load Time sometimes goes by a techie acronym— TTLB or "Total Time until Last Byte is received," and it's fairly uncomplicated: load time, fast or slow, is said to be the determining factor in a consumer's perception of site performance. Poor site performance means weakened brand trustworthiness and appeal, and can affect Bounce Rate and Site Abandonment Rate.

- Bounce Rate and Abandonment Rate appear similar but they're not. Bounce Rate is the percentage of visitors to your site who leave after viewing only one page or (to some analysts) in under five seconds. A high Bounce Rate generally means the site isn't meeting visitors' expectations.

- The (Transaction) Abandonment Rate measures very specific site real estate, usually the cart and checkout pages. A high rate of this sort means there were more people intending to buy (by adding merchandise to their carts) than people who actually purchased relative to an industry average.

As metrics have evolved, so has marketers' notion of "conversion" as something worthy of exhaustive attention. At the heart of this reappraisal is the on-demand consumer, who might very well want to do anything but buy, but she wants to do it efficiently.

- The Task Completion Rate is based on a survey about site visitors' primary purpose for visiting and stated ability to complete that purpose—measured over several months.
- Browse-to-Buy Ratio is a product level metric enabling the marketer to see the number of views a product has had and the number of orders of that product—online and/or offline.
- The View-Through metric has gained a foothold because it recognizes that the path from exposure to conversion can move across many environments and media. It shows brands the corollaries between a consumer's exposure to a campaign, web site, article, review or other information and an eventual interaction with the brand (by buying, requesting further information, subscribing to an online newsletter, etc.).
- RSS Adoption Rate is a measurement of how many consumers signed up for your branded feed of information and special offers because they wanted this on-demand service.

Foundational PERSONAL metrics are intimately tied to just how intimate relations are between a brand and its consumers.

- Gauging how much a consumer feels valued by a brand can be done through some form of Consumer Satisfaction metric, often in combination with another metric, such as Rate of Return visits. (The American Customer Satisfaction Index (ACSI) is also a leading economic indicator.)
- Registered Accounts, because they require extra effort, are a reliable metric of good consumer personal experiences with a brand.

- Return Visits per Unique Individual is determined by "average visits per visitor" during the course of a month. Major portals often top the charts for return visits during a month, followed by social networking sites, so brands should strive to bring users back with some of what these sites offer.

As the personal experience takes its cue from the icitizen motivation to achieve some measure of fame, it needs metrics that bring individuals into sharp focus, both in their interaction with a brand and with others they can influence. VIP treatment can't happen until the VIPs are identified and their behaviors and attitudes measured. Several emerging metrics enable this:

- Profile Extension: Profiles have been around since the dawn of e-commerce, but a high percentage of profiles containing sociographic or psychographic information are of greater value to the brand.
- The Visitor Investment Index (a.k.a. Visitor Interaction Score) is based on points given to particular actions taken by consumers on a web site over a period of time. Bonus points go to those visitors who perform multiple actions that indicate they have a personal investment in the site, e.g. storing their own content; managing their orders or calendars, wishlists, etc.
- Mobile Opt-In Rate: If high, this is a good measure of consumers' willingness to permit brands to enter their personal lives, and can help identify brand fans.
- Advanced Attitudinal Measures help marketers move beyond customer satisfaction to collecting attitudes about the brand that provide insight into the brand's equity for individuals or segments—whether they have brand awareness, brand preference or brand "insistence."
- Percent UGC (User-Generated Content) readily identifies the

high-value individual brand fans by the most labor-intensive type of activity.

- On-Site Influencer Score derives from the monitoring of reviewers on a site to determine who are the power reviewers capable of influencing others' purchase patterns and brand involvement, and deserving of special treatment.
- Social Media Index is a weighted, blended score taken from several social media tools such as business cards (LinkedIn), mini-updates (Twitter, Pownce, etc.), blogs, etc. The more activity on these tools/platforms, i.e., connections, mentions, links, the higher the score. SMI can be useful in identifying influentials in the environment beyond a brand's web site.

ENGAGING metrics focus on consumers' emotional involvement with a brand. Though easily as old as advertising itself, the following foundational metrics have been given a serious boost recently by the marketing industry's interest in arriving at a standard definition of engagement—consumer involvement with a brand as opposed to passive exposure to it.

- Site Visit Duration has evolved into an important performance measure of web sites, and is now used to rank sites by companies such as Nielsen/NetRatings and comScore/Media Metrix. Though an improvement over the old "page view" metric for site ranking in the age of pageless AJAX and streaming video, it does not measure the determinants of site duration or the types of user emotional states that might result.
- Content Group Duration measures which areas of a site are most attractive to visitors. The content groups are analyzed for possible cross-promotions, and analyzed over time to interpret content popularity.
- Unique Visitors measures the number of visitors to a site,

whether they visited one time or many during a specific period of time, and is based on unique cookie ID's. This metric helps brands indicate the breadth of their market appeal, rather than the depth of their appeal to individual consumers. If paired with number of visits, this metric can indicate whether your site is worth visiting.

- Opt-In—to an email newsletter, mobile messages, etc.—is a great way to segment users who want more interaction with a brand.
- Impressions are the number of times an ad has been shown to a visitor of a search engine, a publisher site, the retailer's own site, etc. Counting ad impressions was standardized in 2004 in order to establish consistent and accurate online advertising measurements across publishers and ad serving technologies.

Emerging metrics for an Engaging experience include the following:
- Sentiment is a key component of a brand's buzz and can be measured through content mining for positive or negative expressions. Nielsen BuzzMetrics scans text for subjective language that might indicate the author's opinions about a topic, brand, issue or company.
- Purchase Intent is a self-reported measurement of consumers' intention to purchase, and is used to help determine the extent to which campaigns, coupons or other marketing initiatives (considering their content, frequency, reach, etc.) made consumers more inclined to buy, which is verifiable online, offline or both.
- Favoriting/Social Bookmarking is one of the newer indices of a brand's popularity and ability to be part of the consumer conversation. Consumers use sites like Digg or del.icio.us

to share material they find interesting for the benefit of a wider audience.

- Content Consumption is also known as Depth of Site Visited, a measure that indicates a brand's success at pulling a consumer through its web site by engaging them with rich media, fresh content, calls to action, etc.
- Duration-Satisfaction is an improvement over Site Visit Duration inasmuch as it also measures consumer satisfaction during that stay.

NETWORKED **metrics track the movement of a brand's message across various media and through the world of interpersonal digital communications.**

Foundational metrics include the following:

- Send to a Friend is a measurable activity on-site or in-banner that represents one of the earliest forms of social networking or viral online.
- Non-Search Engine-Referred Traffic helps marketers determine the source of their site visitors, thereby enabling them to optimize their advertising or sponsorship mix.

- Share of Voice (SOV) allows brands to understand how much of a bite they're taking out of the consumer space—e.g., how many consumers are exposed to their advertising and messaging compared to competitor messaging.

Though still being defined by the industry, the emerging Networked metrics are focused most closely on the activities and social networks that are changing the game for brands, and are growing rapidly in number and sophistication:

- Attributed Conversions are a measure of the number of consumer conversions reasonably attributable to an influential individual due to her valuable reviews, a social networking profile incorporating branded entertainment that links to a product page, etc.
- Aggregated Postings Volume is an on-site indicator of a brand's potential network reach, as it measures the flux in the number of consumer postings—ratings and reviews, comments, etc—over a period of time.
- Buzz Monitoring is a sophisticated blend of social media metrics used to determine a brand's "health" and reputation in advance of problems and as a way to glean insights into consumers' conversations about brands.
- Net Promoter Score uses the question, "How likely is it that you would recommend us to a friend or colleague?" to segment a brand's consumers into promoters, passives and detractors. Subtracting the percent of detractors from the percent of promoters helps firms create a bottom-line metric akin to net worth or net profit.
- Pass-along Rate indicates the "viral" value of an ad campaign.
- Content Propagation is a measurement of the dissemination or reach of a brand's assets through the consumer as medium.

Consider the O.P.E.N. metrics system as it's applied to a couple of examples:

A jewelry retailer whose most important consumer segment is affluent boomers has decided to optimize the on-demand experience. Through research the brand has learned that its big spenders are already devoted to the brand and just want to make purchases with greater ease. The Open Rate of its recent email campaign is higher than average because it announces a new convenience for event-related gift giving. This convenience comes in the form of a calendar widget that reminds consumers of important relatives' birthdays and anniversaries. The widget itself, though, is slow to catch hold. Is it possible that too few have actually seen and tried it, even if they clicked through to the jeweler's site from the email describing the widget and from an accompanying banner ad? Measuring Bounce Rate will help determine if this scenario is the problem. Measuring the Task Completion Rate for consumers setting up the widget will shed light on how many uploaded their important dates. Finally, measuring a lift in RFM tied directly to the widget will be a snap because traffic from the widget to the site's checkout can be tagged and tracked.

An apparel retailer has millennials and X'ers as a target market and is optimizing its networked experience due to the brand's consumer expectations and the competition's high visibility on Facebook and Bebo. The brand has recently sponsored a video mashup competition on YouTube and Revver as well as its own retail site, which had a very respectable rate of participation. But measuring consumers' "Content Propagation" only starts with the number of videos submitted. It also means measuring their Pass-along Rate—which indicates how many videos were shared with participants' friends, and measuring buzz, the Talk Dispersion

the brand has affected as a result of the campaign. Has the brand moved the needle? And, if so, can it point definitively to improved customer acquisition? Using a buzz monitoring service will help determine if there was a meaningful increase in customer awareness of the brand.

Beyond the O.P.E.N. metrics system itself, there are three guiding principles for measuring success in a web-made world:

Define your objectives. As Forrester Research's Christine Overby puts it, "Marketers are looking for silver bullet metrics on their dashboards, but it's not that easy. You have to identify your marketing mandate first and then identify the corresponding metrics to place on the dashboard." Without objectives or desired "outcomes," a multiplatform campaign, community site update or new RSS feeds cannot be measured as either providing value to the consumer or to the brand.

Accept the current lack of metrics standardization. Recall that the old standard for the ad industry—gross rating points (GRPs)— was never more than a proxy measure, and empirically challenged at that. Marketers accepted the correlation between ads and sales was causal: the detergent spot, given enough frequency and reach, would yield X sales, right? Today, marketers are more attuned to the incremental steps between awareness and purchase. They can measure nearly all of those steps without always knowing which should be weighted more heavily—in-game advertising or the web site Click-Through Rate—unless correlated with specific conversion objectives. Accepting the relative nature of online metrics when stacked up against traditional metrics like GRPs is particularly important because cross-platform measurement is costly, complicated and not yet widely adopted by retailers.

Aspire to integrate media measurement whenever possible. To measure the impact of ads everywhere they're viewed, NBC's Total Audience Media Interactive research tool provides advertisers with cross-media data on various broadcast and cable outlets, online (through streaming video and downloads) and mobile. Post-purchase surveys ask consumers which touchpoints had an effect on their buying decision—and at what juncture on their purchase path—and can separate causality from mere correlation, particularly when combined with the Browse-to-Buy Ratio. (Be sure to account for the exaggerated importance consumers invariably ascribe to mass media campaigns in such surveys.)

Ours is an era of spiraling expectations of marketing accountability; the more we can measure, the more we are compelled to measure. But even if data is king, marketers shouldn't become its indentured servants. This open branding era can be the richest in both data-driven consumer insights and marketing ROI by implementing those metrics best suited to one of the four consumer experiences, each of which comes with its own business objective.

17:
Opening Jitters

As brands adopt an open worldview, the blogosphere and mainstream media have been quick to expose the rewards, but also, and most sensationally, the risks of the expansive online environment. Online search makes available indefinitely an enthralling and sprawling record of everything from rash experimentalism to unwieldy consumer/brand co-creation. Like the genie in a bottle, once it's out there, it's hard to contain again.

Some of the most memorable tales of open branding gone awry involve brand hijacking—when consumers appropriate a brand for their own purposes, in ways often not intended by the brand itself but that create or solidify a niche following. Brand hijacking predates the social web, but the digital frontier has intensified and complicated the output.

Other open branding cautionary tales feature culture jamming, which subverts the brand's communications as a critique of consumerism itself. Chevy Tahoe's 2006 online mashup campaign achieved iconic culture jamming status when some of the over 30,000 videos created at a dedicated web site came from environmental detractors using biting humor as a weapon against gas-guzzling SUVs.

Many open brand cautionary tales do have happy endings, but their admonitions remain clear: the journey—the participatory contract with consumers—can't be undertaken lightly. When brands commit to serving the social web's four essential consumer experiences, they also expose themselves to a range of reputation, legal and ethical risks. This is such new territory that the courts, the media and public opinion are still wrangling over what's right, what's wrong, what's allowed and what's not. Being cognizant of the complexities in this environment is the best way to avoid becoming a victim of its darker side.

IP ON THE RUN

U.S. copyright, trademark and patent laws are struggling to keep up with waves of new technologies offering myriad ways to create, access and alter new and existing content. At issue: who owns what, and how to protect the creators, the creations (and even the naïve infringers).

Online content currently under copyright can be "screen scraped," fragmented, mashed up and linked to in a million new ways in a million digital nooks and crannies. Yet much of this appropriation or infringement is either unwitting or premised on "fair use" and the belief in the free flow of information.

The concept of "fair use"—which allows the limited reproduction of copyrighted materials for criticism, commentary, reporting and the like—has been given a boost by the Freedom and Innovation Revitalizing U.S. Entrepreneurship (FAIR USE) Act of 2007. The FAIR USE Act, a bill introduced into Congress in February 2007, attempts to loosen restrictions on consumers imposed by the 1998 Digital Millennium Copyright Act (DMCA)—particularly when using copyrighted material in their homes. (The DMCA bans circumventing Digital Rights Management technologies placed on consumer electronics devices to control the pirating of copyrightable works—but in doing so also limits the basic sharing of content among legal users, such as library patrons.) In some circumstances, the FAIR USE Act might also provide some protection for digital toolmakers whose inventions have non-infringing purposes.

Currently, web sites, internet service providers and search engines hosting or linking to copyrighted material without the IP owner's permission or without having paid a fee can be served a DMCA takedown notice, and few of these notices are disputed; most companies simply comply, which largely protects them from further liability. To proactively protect themselves from liability, some of the most popular sites for content sharing are relying on automatic filtering technology to detect copyright infringement. Companies such as MySpace have licensed technology that checks music uploads by its community against a database of copyrighted music. Other companies are developing technologies

> The DCMA's "safe harbor" provisions protect online service providers (OSPs) from liability for information posted or transmitted by subscribers if they swiftly remove or disable access to the material identified in a copyright holder's complaint.
>
> In order to qualify for safe harbor protection, an OSP must:
> - have no knowledge of, or financial benefit from, the infringing activity
> - provide proper notification of its policies to users
> - retain a publicly-identified agent, who must be registered with the U.S. copyright office, to deal with copyright complaints

for identifying and removing poor-quality copies of video or audio that are likely the result of fraudulent uploads.

In the spirit of open source, many creators are making their copyrighted material available to others via Creative Commons (CC) licensing, through which creators can allow greater use while still maintaining their preferred rights to, say, attribution. CC license owners—like some Flickr users and the filmmakers behind the 2006 open source short film *Elephants Dream*—place a notice of "some rights reserved" on their work (as opposed to the traditional copy-right notice, "all rights reserved"). This open source take on intel-lectual property rights is fueling inspired collaboration and sparking wider dissemination of (and recognition for) the works of authors and musicians, filmmakers, artists and scientists around the world— some of which can now fairly be put in the service of brands.

The digital marketplace suffers from a double-edged sword when it comes to new technology patents. On the one hand, new software patents can be hard to come by because of the vast amount of easily posted and searched content generated by thinkers and dreamers about possible future technologies. These references might be construed as "prior art"—content that describes or anticipates an invention, the existence of which can invalidate a patent claim or prevent a patent claim from issuing in the first place. And it can be found in bytes and bits all over the internet.

On the other hand, some software patents (especially those granted in the earlier days of the internet), are perceived as being so broad and encompassing that they might limit future creative iterations in broad categories of innovation. When such patents are ultimately granted, as in the case of Friendster's social media technology patent or Amazon's patent for "one-click" payment systems, they allow the patent holder to take legal action against a wide range of competitors large and small, putting a chill on innovation in fast-moving categories such as social networking and e-commerce.

To help safeguard the value of software innovation efforts against the risk of costly legal battles over broad technology patents, software industry leaders funded the launch of the Open Innovation Network (OIN) to increase access to key patents for software collaborators, and to work closely with the U.S. Patent & Trademark Office to improve the application-examination process.

The open brand should constantly monitor evolving IP laws (and lawsuits) in order to understand what material can be manipulated and shared—and how—and to keep its consumers informed and protected as well.

THE BRAND FAN HAS TWO FACES

Marketers today face competition from consumers—specifically, the amateurs behind the consumer-generated content boom. Learn from the competition? Good idea. Impersonate them?

Not such a good idea. In Vegas, they call it shill. In politics and theater, it's called an audience plant. In digital marketing, they call it flogging for "fake blogging," or sock puppeting, when a fake persona is adopted to discuss or comment on oneself or one's work, particularly in an online discussion group or on a blog. And in PR, campaigns that pretend to be naturally generated by nonprofessionals are known as astroturfing.

In December 2006, the Federal Trade Commission made a "no-action" decision regarding whether a company's failure to disclose when paid agents are used to promote products to their peers might be "unfair and deceptive." The FTC will be taking action on a case-by-case basis. The decision came after the advertising and marketing watchdog group Commercial Alert asked the FTC to investigate buzz marketing and its occasionally deceptive tactics.

More than a year before the FTC's ruling, The Word of Mouth Marketing Association (WOMMA) was already promoting an Ethics Code to its 300+ membership of marketers and advertisers. The code is based on three simple principles of transparency:

1. Say whom you're speaking for (e.g., a brand)
2. Say what you believe (not what you've been paid to say)
3. Never obscure your identity (by pretending to be, say, a local college barfly when you're really a hired marketing agent for a beer brand)

Some of the biggest brands have been caught faking it. Jim and Laura's "WalMarting Across America" RV adventure was documented on a relentlessly sunny flog for the company—and eventually revealed as a PR stunt. The crazy bride cutting off her hair on YouTube was, it turned out, a Canada Sunsilk effort. Sony launched a flog to promote its PSP (Sony PlayStation Portable) for holiday 2006. The site portrayed its creator as "Charlie," an ordinary kid who was supposedly blogging, dancing and rapping to convince his friend's parents to buy his pal a PSP for Christmas.

A little digging revealed that Charlie's blog was registered to an agency hired by Sony to create the site. When more than 600 posts by outraged visitors appeared on the flog's forum, Sony Computer Entertainment America finally posted this mea culpa: "…Guess we were trying to be just a little too clever. From this point forward, we will just stick to making cool products, and use this site to give you nothing but the facts on the PSP."

Lesson learned. The open brand should stick with the real deal: word-of-mouth support spread transparently by its most authentic enthusiasts.

THE NAKED "TRUTH"

Bloggers are in the business of telling it as they see it, and brands sometimes bear the brunt of their biases. Likewise, consumer-posted reviews or feedback, while generally helpful, can also be inaccurate, profane and mean-spirited. But once brands publicly commit to soliciting opinions, either through their own community forums or on-site ratings and reviews, they have to resist the temptation, as Johnny Mercer once lyricized, to "accentuate the positive and eliminate the negative."

Negative reviews and posts are a natural part of a fair and free-wheeling exchange with and among consumers, and have to remain visible, in all their bruising glory. Besides, they can be the source of the brand's most valuable consumer insights, and can arguably build brand credibility over time more effectively than a set of purely (and suspiciously) positive reviews. But brands do have rights—and ways to keep the conversation constructive.

Dell had a "look, don't touch" policy with regard to bloggers in 2005, right about the time Jeff Jarvis (media consultant, interactive journalism professor and founder of *Entertainment Weekly*) wrote a series of devastating posts about his PC on his BuzzMachine blog. "Dell Hell"—the title of one of Jarvis's rants—metastasized in the blogosphere, then moved to traditional media, but two years later, the company's consumer relations have dramatically changed, primarily due to the creation of the very thing the company had avoided: a corporate/public forum for the people's ideas. IdeaStorm, an online community where Dell consumers offer ideas on Dell's products and services and vote on the best of them, has not only impacted consumer confidence but—as an ideal open branding scenario—has led to actual product improvement: Dell now offers Linux not just in servers and workstations but also in desktops and laptops.

If an organization edits a citizen's contribution, the organization might expose itself to a lawsuit claiming libel or copyright infringement. That's why online Terms and Conditions for use (a.k.a. Ts & Cs) come in handy; they can require posters to agree to having their content edited or removed, and shift liability from the publishing entity to the content creator. They also set standards for community behavior, and provide fair warning that users might be blocked from contributing if they violate the agreed-to terms.

Though difficult to police or enforce without the participation of other users who report abuse (or an in-house online policy team that can take down content), Ts & Cs can bar users from submitting false, defamatory, abusive, obscene, threatening, racially offensive, sexually explicit or illegal material—ultimately reducing the burden of liability for the brand or company hosting the user-generated content.

Likewise, while some online advocates promote anonymous posting as a form of free speech, for brands, requiring mandatory log-in before contributing falls in the category of an ounce of prevention trumping a pound of cure. Along with Ts & Cs, mandatory log-in can help protect brands from renegade user behavior.

Brands can also steer consumers in a positive way, by prompting topics for discussion that can benefit the community at large, as well as the brand. What's good for the engaged consumer is good for the brand. The people behind the prompting and listening occupy some of the newest positions in marketing—Toyota has a Corporate Manager of Consumer Generated Media—and some of the oldest but increasingly valued positions, including consumer affairs and public relations.

Ultimately, the community itself is the most effective tool for shaping and policing user-generated content. When empowered with reporting mechanisms, users freely report objectionable content to the proper authorities (often, the online policy enforcers employed by many large content sites). Users also vote online with simple "Was this information helpful?" feedback polls that can drive poorly ranked content to the bottom of the bin.

In short, transparent (but requisite) policies and log-ins and a self-policing user base can be the best tools for brands seeking to enable consumer- (or employee-) generated content without suffering collateral damage in the process.

CROWDS KNOW BEST

The "wisdom of crowds" theory, put forth in James Surowiecki's 2004 book, of the same name, argues for the uncanny ability of large groups of relatively uninformed people to guess or calculate more accurate answers than those of individual experts.

While technology is hardly necessary to capture the wisdom of crowds, the internet is the perfect testing ground for collective knowledge formation. Surowiecki believes that, when four conditions are met—independence of members from each other, diversity, decentralization of power, and skillful and fair aggregation of opinions—such group knowledge processes can improve the performance of businesses, marketplaces and even governments.

In the past, teams of market researchers and business analysts have been responsible for conducting research, formulating insights and applying this knowledge to a brand's product development, marketing communications and business practices. The social web now automatically offers such insights—for those willing to comb its layers and aggregate its two different kinds of knowledge. The first kind is from credentialed, deep subject matter experts, whose knowledge is often accrued through formal education and over a lifetime. The second kind is consumer knowledge, based on personal experiences and personal research. Consumer knowledge outweighs expert knowledge online in increasingly exponential proportions.

The relevant, accurate output of massively distributed amateurs and professionals-turned-collaborators is surprisingly good. Consider Wikipedia, the world's largest collaborative encyclopedia. With six million entries at the close of 2006, and with at least some portions translated (by volunteers) into more than 250 languages, Wikipedia is an open branding smash hit. Part of its success lies in the ability of users not only to create entries, but also to edit and correct entries written by others. Even with its somewhat fluid accuracy, occasional partisan rants and potential for textual vandalism, Wikipedia is considered an exemplar of the best and brightest of crowd-created information.

However, as Wikipedia has become not just a source of reference material but a real-time news source as well (*The New York Times* reported on July 1, 2007 that 250 of the "most recent changes to the English-language Wikipedia were made in the last 60 seconds"), its editorial processes have become a bit less democratic, a bit more bureaucratic.

About 1200 English-language administrators have extra content management rights, including the ability to "semiprotect" an entry or even put it under "full protection" in order to shut out vandalism. The latter action was required after the accuracy of the Wikipedia entry for David Chase (creator of *The Sopranos*) was whacked by angry fans seeking revenge for the HBO series' quizzical finale. It goes to show that even the wisest of crowds need a bit of control.

The Hollywood Stock Exchange (HSX) is another source of aggregated amateur "expertise." Its over 1.5 million registered traders use fake money to buy and sell "shares" in movies and stars. This virtual stock exchange has generated box office predictions so consistently accurate that the studios study HSX when deciding which films and stars to promote most heavily—and which to leave on the cutting room floor.

For marketers facing the unwieldy communal wisdom of their own consumers, the rewards of allowing crowds to rate, review, share, opine and define outweigh the risks of giving them the free reign to do so, and the effort required to organize and assess the wisdom. In time, most brands come to realize that real pearls of wisdom always surface. As Shakespeare wrote (in *The Merchant of Venice*), "At length the truth will out."

18:

Rules of the Open Road

A distillation of some of the key themes for opening your brand.

[The Future of Brands is Open]

→ Rally your organization to shift its worldview from closed to open.

→ Steward your brand by focusing on a critical new asset: the creative consumer.

→ Embrace the five reasons to open up your brand:
  • Revenue from niche audiences and long-tail consumers
  • ROI from more effectively targeted marketing
  • R&D from consumers eager to share ideas and opinions
  • Relevance to the participatory ethos of the social web
  • Relationships with online consumers who can become your media and marketing

→ Be O.P.E.N.—on-demand, personal, engaging and networked.

→ Put technologists in your marketing innovation inner circle.

→ Support online consumers' three key social web behaviors: creating, sharing and influencing.

[The Rise of the iCitizen]

→ Know your icitizens—those creative consumers with sufficient expertise, passion and transparency to distinguish themselves from the rest of the online population.

→ Enlist the four motivations of the icitizenry in the service of your brand, which include the desire to:
  • achieve digital competence, even mastery
  • act collectively or belong to and engage with a community of people like them
  • effect cultural change
  • attain some measure of celebrity or peer recognition

→ Create or provide digital DIY tools that enable competence-seeking icitizens to become proficient online, collectivism-minded and celebrity-motivated icitizens to self-express and influence their networks, and change-motivated icitizens to make a difference.

→ Treat celebrity- and change-motivated elite icitizens as real individualists, with the potential to become personal brands, intimately tied to your brand.

→ Mine the web for the next face or voice of your brand. It will increase your relevance and ensure your brand's role in the social web's diverse spheres of influence.

→ Digital millennials' social networks are vast. Increase your brand's buzz and reach by being authentic, original and entertaining, and by seeking their involvement and forfeiting control.

→ Make consumer-initiated mobile marketing a priority, particularly if your target market includes digital millennials.

→ Understand that a brand's new job is to cultivate a love triangle by facilitating interaction between consumers and communities and identifying their shared passion.

→ Transform your marketing mindset from purchase funnel to social media fish to support the volume and diversity of creating, sharing and influencing activities throughout the consumer journey.

→ In an era of declining deference to traditional authorities, including the brand, regard the propensity of your customer base to recommend products and services to others as one of the single largest measures of your brand equity.

[Inside the Open Brand]

→ Provide four types of interconnected consumer experiences, anchored by the social web's behavioral continuums: anonymity to notoriety, and consumption to production:
  • The On-Demand Experience: characterized by efficiency, ease, control, findability and instantaneousness

- The Personal Experience: characterized by acknowledgement, dialogue, customization, privilege and popularity
- The Engaging Experience: characterized by participation, belonging, immersion, entertainment and inspiration
- The Networked Experience: characterized by self-expression, ego gratification, portability, community and meaningful change

→ Find your sweet spot within the open brand framework by understanding your consumers' expectations for interaction, and your competitive landscape of openness, and then prioritizing one or more of the four essential consumer experiences of the social web.

[Getting to Open]

→ Measure your open branding success by aligning your business objectives with the consumer experiences you deem most important, then employing metrics best suited to either on-demand, personal, engaging or networked.

→ Mix foundational and emerging metrics as a way to capture the most important insights into an online population in transition. Test and learn.

→ Define your objectives so your analytics data will be actionable; don't be deterred by the current lack of metrics standardization; and try to integrate diverse media measurement whenever possible.

→ Empower your online community to police itself with reporting mechanisms for bad behavior and ranking questions such as "Was this review helpful?"

→ Steer consumers in a positive way by prompting topics that can benefit the community at large. Resist the urge to control the dialogue.

→ Manage the naked "truth" (opinions as well as facts) of consumers and employees with online Terms and Conditions, which set the ground rules for appropriate use of online resources.

→ Require users to log in before they post comments to reduce the likelihood of inappropriate content being posted anonymously.

→ Study the icitizenry's "research"—their published experiences of and opinions about your brand. However anecdotal and generally lacking in specialized study, this content is free, current, candid and voluminous.

Appendix

Open Lingo

Alerts

Emails sent to users who want to be notified of updates on everything from sales to sporting events to mortgage rate fluctuations.

Application Programming Interface (API)

A set of routines, protocols and tools for building software applications that are compatible with an operating environment such as MS-Windows, and for requesting lower-level services performed by that operating system. Although APIs are designed for programmers, they are ultimately good for users because they guarantee that all programs using a common API will have similar interfaces.

Astroturfing

Public relations campaigns that pretend to be spontaneously generated by the public but are not.

Avatar

A virtual identity created by users to represent themselves in a virtual reality or computer game. Popularized by Neal Stephenson, the author of the cyber novel *Snow Crash*, and from a Hindu word for the personification of deities or entities. Avatars' first use was in multiuser domains (MUDs).

Blogosphere

The world of weblogs and blog-related web sites.

Bookmarking

Creating a link to a web page to make it easy to find again. Bookmarks help users store, classify, share and search for material. Social bookmarking is not tied to a specific computer or browser but rather is web-based and stresses the usefulness of the bookmark for others.

Citizen journalism

Also known as "participatory journalism," the concept of non-journalists collecting, reporting, analyzing and disseminating news and information.

Closed brand

Brands that cling to tight control of marketing to ensure a specific public image; they engage consumers at arms' length with traditional media in an attempt to choreograph the brand experience. The opposite of an open brand!

Consumer-Generated Media (CGM)	Experiences created by customers; often funny, sometimes edgy, CGM in all its forms might be the single most important driver of the open branding revolution. Also known as Consumer-Created Content.
Cookie	A small text file of information sent by a server to a web browser and then sent back unchanged by the browser each time it accesses that server. Used for authenticating, tracking and maintaining specific information about users, such as site preferences and the contents of their electronic shopping carts.
Creative Commons	A non-profit organization that offers flexible and varied copyright licenses intended to let people under certain conditions copy and distribute all kinds of creative works from blogs to films and songs.
Customer Relationship Management (CRM)	A program used to manage customer contacts.
Flashmob	A group of strangers that gathers together briefly in public to share a common experience based on instructions sent via digital devices.
Flog	Fake blog, often created by an agency to look as if consumers contributed; almost always "outed" by vigilant bloggers.
Guided navigation	Search results arranged on a web site to show all the helpful ways to refine a search and explore further; based on metadata.
HTML or Hypertext Markup Language	Authoring software language used to create web pages and automatically generated taxonomies.
IM or Instant messaging	Real-time chat; usually a free downloadable program and the online communication of choice of digital millennials.

Long tail	A term coined by Chris Anderson to describe a well-known statistical distribution. Used to describe products that are not widely popular but that, if aggregated, can compete for market share with blockbusters.
Macrotrends	Trends that pass the STEEP test: they have social, technological, economic, environmental and political implications.
Mashups	Two or more sets of data combined online to create a new entity; often used with software, music or video.
M-commerce or Mobile commerce	Wireless e-commerce where consumers use their mobile devices to purchase goods and services.
Micro-community	A web site whose members share information about specific interests, concerns or experiences.
Network effects	Effects that cause the value of a product to its consumers to increase if it is more widely used.
Open rate	A measure of how many people on an email list open a particular email campaign.
Open source	Started as the notion of a free program with source code available to the general public for use and/ or modification; programmers improve upon the software code collaboratively and share changes with the community. Many refer to its rise as the "open source movement."
Opt-in	Consumers consent to have promotions and other information sent to them.
Out of Home (OOH)	Advertising that reaches consumers while they are out of their homes, via billboards, for example.
Pay Per Click (PPC)	Search engine marketing used by advertisers, who pay a set amount each time their ad is clicked by a sales prospect.

Personas	Composite identities assigned by marketers to consumer segments to bring the latter to life; possess personality traits and, generally, purchasing agendas.
Portal	Web pages that act as entry points to the internet.
Rich Internet Applications (RIA)	A web application that resembles a traditional desktop application—with functionality like "drag and drop"—by transferring some of the processing to the web client (rather than the server). Typically runs in a web browser.
Rich media	A broad range of digital interactive media that exhibits dynamic motion. Can be downloadable, or can be embedded on a web page.
RSS feed	Rich Site Summary or Really Simple Syndication; a way for web sites to summarize content, such as news articles, in order to make it available in a different view.
Screen scraping	Acquiring data displayed on screen by capturing the text manually with the copy command or via software. Web pages are constantly being screen scraped in order to save meaningful data (originally written for human consumption) for later use. In order to perform scraping automatically, software must be used that is written to recognize specific semantic data structures.
Search Engine Marketing (SEM)	The marketing of a web site via search engines, by improving rank in organic listings, purchasing paid listings or a combination of both.
SERP	Search engine results pages.
Search Engine Optimization (SEO)	The process of improving the volume and quality of traffic to a web site from search engines' organic search results.
Searchandizing	Using search on a web site to promote certain products when certain keywords are used.

Share of Voice (SOV)	A brand's advertising footprint expressed as a percentage of a total market or market segment in a given time period. Often defined in terms of expenditure.
Sock Puppeting	Adopting a fake persona in order to discuss or comment on oneself or one's work, particularly in an online discussion group or on a blog.
Short Message Service (SMS)	Text messaging service on mobile phones.
Swarming	The act of organizing spontaneous get-togethers via cell phone.
Tag cloud	A cluster of words used to describe available information; a blog or site might make certain words larger and bolder to indicate the most popular topics searched by users. Also called a weighted list.
Talk dispersion	One of the phenomena studied by buzz monitoring services. Their content mining capabilities identify where conversations take place and how they are dispersed, or how they spread.
Taxonomy	The core component of information architecture, taxonomy has two aspects—view and structure—and is derived from analysis of usage patterns and information flow, and based on standards and guidelines. It helps sites present content logically by grouping information into topics and assigning intuitive labeling.
Threaded discussion	A running commentary of messages between two or more people in a discussion group.
Twittering	Twitter is the brand name of a social networking and micro-blogging service that utilizes instant messaging, SMS and web interfaces. Other micro-blogging services include Jaiku and Pownce.
Video scraping	The video version of screen scraping.

Viral	Short for viral marketing; a marketing message that gets passed along in significant (sometimes massive) numbers, often accruing impressions much higher than traditional ad placement.
Virally communal	Communal by virtue of word-of-mouth circulation.
Web 2.0	The second generation of internet functions, mostly collaborative in nature; includes social networking, wikis, video sharing and folksonomies.
Web applications	Applications that are accessed via the web and can be updated without installing new software. Web apps generate web documents in a standard format such as HTML/XHTML that are supported by common browsers.
Web form	A form on a web page where users can enter in data that is typically found in paper forms but that can be sent to the server for processing. Forms can be used to send and retrieve data.
Widget	A small reusable portion of code that brings in live content to a web page.
Wiki	A collaborative web site comprised of the perpetual collective work of many authors.

Acknowledgments

In the spirit of openness, this book was an enormous collaboration. More than that, it could never have come to fruition without the intellectual generosity and skills of many Resource Interactive clients, digital marketing executives and advertising friends, and most notably, our talented colleagues.

This project began with a "call for open participation" to the more than 250 Resource Interactive associates—an open invitation to research, discuss and debate the fast-moving trends in social media and the implications for brands of every sort. It goes without saying that while "opening" has its immense rewards, it is not without difficulty, as we learned firsthand. While we found the brainpower and additional hands on deck exhilarating and supportive, it was also challenging and time-consuming to review, consider and evaluate points of view from so many different types of experts. Dozens of versions of chapters were created. Tens of thousands of words were written and sidelined. Ultimately, synthesizing all contributions into a single voice and point of view became our top (and toughest) job. In the final result, it's difficult for us to ascertain who wrote which line—co-creation in its finest form.

We are deeply indebted to our core team of Sara Saldoff, Laura Bergheim and Karen Watts for their extraordinary editorial guidance, contributions and patience as the narrative took shape amidst a rapidly changing social media landscape. We appreciate the honest feedback from Nancy Kramer, Edd Johns, Molly Metzger, Karen Scholl, Scott Holley, Ann Mooney, John Kadlic, Mila Goodman, Nancy Koors and Karla Allen. Additionally, we are grateful to Christopher Celeste for his provocative insights and constructive review comments.

A gracious thank you to Holly Davis for organizing and synthesizing our experts' interviews and Gail Sech and Deb Rycus for identifying the lingo you should know. A special thanks to Susan Ashley, Emily Miller, Rick Smith, Tyler Snouffer, Rick Kleban and Lisa Bownas for helping to draw conclusive insights about the evolutionary imperative for measurement. We owe our appreciation to Chris Berk, Dennis Bajec, Mark Hillman and Laura Evans for helping us test our theories by developing hypothetical Open Brand Makeovers. Thanks also to Dawn Egelston, Jay Donavan, Joey Zornes, Lara Lebeiko, Mark Scholl, Chris Heine, Jessica Reid, Marti Bledsoe, Michael Stephenson, Bob Hale, Tarrance Jackson, Stephanie Jones, Mike Ebright, Gabe Shultz and our tireless research assistant, Sarah Song. Last, the message of this book came to life through the graphic design. For his obsessive commitment to his craft, we applaud Terry Rohrbach. We also thank him for countless cover designs, which were ultimately voted upon by a crowd of 650 attendees at ATG's annual conference, wielding their mobile devices.

We recognize how fortunate we are to have clients as both friends and partners whose passions for innovation fuel our creative souls. We are hopeful that the next 25 years will be as adventurous, bold and full of worthy experiments as the first 25 years have been.

A project of this type requires endless late nights and weekends of solitary thinking and writing. Throughout the last year, our friends and family provided enormous emotional support and constant encouragement. We are humbled by their open-mindedness and indebted to their unwavering patience as we pursued this dream.

Index

marketing funnel, new consumer
    journey, 84–87
    medium for cost savings, 89
    people like me, 82
    iCitizen motivations, 57–61
    prosumers, 56
    reshaping consumerism, 52–55
sock puppeting, 179–181
Starwood, 146
Stengel, Richard, 53
Surowiecki, James, 184
swarming, 52

T
tagging, 18, 58
Technorati, 44–45
The Ten Demandments, 8
The Third Wave, 56
The Tipping Point, 54
*The World is Flat: A Brief History of
    the Twentieth Century*, 23
Threadless, 145–146
Toffler, Alvin, *The Third Wave*, 56
trademarks, 175–179
twittering, 52
Typepad, 44–45

U–V
U.S. copyright laws, 175–179

Victoria's Secret, 95
    PINK campaign, 156–157
video scraping, 52
Vox, 44–45

W
Wal-Mart, 115
Warren, Frank, profile, 69
web, 16–17
    brands communicating sense of
        community, 18–19
    brands at risk, 23
    closed brands, 20–21
    opening brands to consumers, 24
    reasons to open brands, 26–27

Web 2.0
    Alpha Openers, 43–45
    online behaviors, 46–48
Webkinz, 154–155
WebMD, 135
Wikipedia, 44–45
Wilder, Scott K., 147

X–Y–Z
YouTube, 44–45

Zillow, 115
Zúniga, Markos Moulitsas, 58, 68

Kelly Mooney has been a consumer-centric marketing innovator for 20 years, and is President of Resource Interactive. She co-authored *The Ten Demandments: Rules to Live by in the Age of the Demanding Consumer* (McGraw-Hill, 2002)—one of the first marketing books to showcase the consumer's perspective. A popular blogger, frequent keynote speaker and expert commentator, her perspectives have been covered by media outlets including *The Wall Street Journal, Business Week, Fortune, Inc., Fast Company, USA Today, Time Digital, People*, CNN, CNBC, CNET, CBS's "The Early Show," *Nikkei Business* (Japan), *Vente à Distance* (France), and *Capital* (Dubai).

Dr. Nita Rollins is a multidisciplinary thinker and Innovation Consultant in the Resource Interactive R&D Lab. She is the author of *Cinaesthetics: The Beautiful, the Ugly, the Sublime and the Kitsch in Post-Metaphysical Film* (2008), and of articles for *Design Management Journal, New Design* (UK), *Innovation: The IDSA Quarterly, Internet Retailer, Cinema Journal* and *Wide Angle*. She earned her Ph.D. in Critical Studies from UCLA's Department of Theater, Film & TV, and has served as Research Fellow at the University of California Humanities Research Institute and the University of Paris III.

Resource Interactive is one of the nation's preeminent independent digital marketing agencies, helping Fortune 500 companies thrive in the evolving internet economy with digital strategy, creative and technology solutions that drive business results. Unique in the industry as female-founded, owned and operated, the company has grown over its 26-year history from its first marketing relationship with Apple to ongoing partnerships with clients such as Procter & Gamble, Hewlett-Packard, Wal-Mart, The Coca-Cola Company, Victoria's Secret and Sherwin-Williams.

All Resource Interactive proceeds from the sales of this book will be donated to One Laptop Per Child (OLPC) which aspires to provide children around the world with new opportunities to explore, experiment and express themselves using the XO laptop, a children's machine designed for "learning learning."